THE GHASTLY GUEST BOOK

THE GHASTLY
GUEST BOOK

Andrew McCall

Illustrations by
Joanna Carrington

St. Martin's Press
New York

To Anthony and Laura
with love

The Perfect Pest and *The Perfect Guest* are reproduced
by kind permission of Mrs L. Buckley from *The
Perfect Hostess*, first published 1931, new edition 1980,
by Debrett's Peerage Limited

Library of Congress Catalog Card Number: 81-83701
ISBN 0-312-32638-6

First Edition

CONTENTS

The Perfect Pest

She merely sent a wire to say
That she was coming down to stay.
She brought a maid of minxsome look
Who promptly quarrelled with the cook.
She smoked, and dropped with ruthless hand
Hot ashes on the Steinway grand.
She strode across the parquet floors
In hobnailed boots from out of doors.
She said the water wasn't hot,
And Jane gave notice on the spot.
She snubbed the wealthy dull relations
From whom my wife had expectations.
She kept her bell in constant peals,
She never was in time for meals.
And when at last with joyful heart
We thrust her in the luggage-cart,
In half an hour she came again,
And said … 'My dear, I've missed the train!'

Adrian Porter

One

MANNERS

'The Graces, the Graces! remember the Graces!'
– Lord Chesterfield to his son (aged sixteen), letter of
January 10, 1749

'The keystone is ... graciousness – a graciousness that
makes people feel at ease with themselves, with you,
with the situation, whatever it may be.' – Charlotte
Ford in her *Book of Modern Manners*, 1980

Is 'graciousness' really the best word? Or does it tend
to conjure up a picture, in the female case, of a
supercilious and condescending monstress, in the
male of either oiliness or impossibly limp wrists? Well,

other writers on behaviour, good and bad, on manners and on etiquette (the need for 'Etiquette Books'
seems to have been most pressing on both sides of the
Atlantic, in the 1880s, and then again in the late
1920s and early '30s) have hit upon other words.
Among these are sympathy, amiability, tact, refine-

ment and even, in one particularly sickening nineteenth-century manual, on how a woman (only) may hope to make a social success of herself, daintiness. But daintiness apart, whether she be Emily Post or Lady Troubridge, whether he be George Washington or Sir Harold Nicolson, what all these pundits are in fact talking about is consideration. And consideration is precisely what every ghastly guest lacks.

Take, for instance, the small matter of teeth. These may be either firmly rooted in the guest's jawbone or removable. If the former, the fourth Earl of Chesterfield's advice to his son, Philip Stanhope (who turned out to be something of a disappointment to the distinguished arbiter of manners and good taste), still holds good. For, says his Lordship, 'a dirty mouth has real ill consequences to the owner … it infallibly causes the decay, as well as the intolerable pain of the teeth; and it is very offensive to his acquaintance, for it will most inevitably stink.' To avoid causing such offence, Lord Chesterfield insists that his son wash his 'teeth the first thing that you do every morning, with a soft sponge and warm water, for four or five minutes, and then wash your mouth five or six times'. Today, a wide variety of gargles, rinses and washes, of tooth brushes, pastes and powders, all help to make oral hygiene a relatively simple matter. Even so, there is still no shortage of people who persist in putting both hosts and fellow-guests off their food with their basilisk breath.

No less reprehensible, on the other hand, are those absent-minded elderly persons, who, when staying with friends or relatives, leave their false teeth in a glass by the basin in a communally used bathroom. For, not only do other people's disembodied false teeth have a curiously disturbing effect on many adults, but to a small child basins are at eye-level, or slightly higher: and it will never be known how many children have woken up screaming, in the dead of night, as a result of having been unexpectedly fixed by the malignant leer of some thoughtless person's quietly soaking set of dentures.

Not such a small matter, then, teeth; nor are hands, feet or armpits, nor even are finger-nails. 'In your person you must be accurately clean,' Lord Chesterfield instructed his son and everyone who has since touched on the subject of filth is agreed that dirtiness is still a serious impediment to attracting the enthusiastic attention of most potential hosts and hostesses. For, as Ethel Frey Cushing pointed out somewhat primly, in 1926, 'We are obliged to take people at their face value upon casually meeting and if they present a polite and well-groomed appearance we become at once interested, and if time is allowed in the acquaintance thus made, the people so equipped will have our first attention in an effort to know them better.' Or, in other words, you are more likely to be asked to lunch, dinner or for the weekend, if you don't smell like a badger or slouch about in clothes heavily spattered with grease spots.

3

As for personal dirtiness, so for dirty habits. 'Every action done in Company ought to be with Some Sign of Respect, to those that are present' was George Washington's first 'Rule of Civility'. Aged thirteen or fourteen at the time, he went on to explain what he had in mind: '... bedew no man's face with your Spittle ... Kill no Vermin as Fleas, lice ticks &c in the Sight of Others ... If you Cough, Sneeze, Sigh or Yawn, do it not Loud, but Privately: and speak not in your Yawning, but put your handkerchief or Hand before your face and turn aside.' Unmentioned – because unmentionable? – by Washington are belches and farts, which should, ideally, be suppressed altogether. Where suppression has proved impossible, they should be ignored, by author – 'Better out than in, ha ha' is a selfish point of view – and audience alike. It was very mean of the seasoned courtier to say, in a loud voice, to the nervous provincial aristocrat, who, at her first royal banquet, broke wind, 'But you mustn't blush, Madame; pretend it was me.'

Vigorous scratching, too, is out; and so are ear, nose, tooth and eye picking. Nor, 'when in Company,' says George Washington, should you 'put ... your Hands to any Part of the Body not usually Discovered.'

All this may seem obvious – as it did to Lord Chesterfield. 'Politeness and good-breeding are ... necessary to make you welcome and agreeable in conversation and common life,' he told his son in 1740. For 'great talents, such as honour, virtue, learning and parts, are above the generality of the world, who neither possess them themselves, nor judge of them rightly in others: but all people are judges of the lesser talents, such as civility, affability, and an obliging, agreeable address and manner; because they feel the good effects of them, as making society easy and pleasing.'

Nine years later he had more to say on the subject. 'There is a natural good-breeding,' he wrote to Philip Stanhope in November 1749, 'which occurs to every man of common-sense, and is practised by every man of common good-nature. This good-breeding is general, independent of modes, and consists in endeavours to please and oblige our fellow-creatures by all good offices short of moral duties. This will be practised by a good-natured American savage as essentially as by the best bred European.' (His Lordship is here referring, of course, to the American Indian, in what he takes to be his natural state of noble savagery.)

But, if the importance of good-breeding (i.e. manners) is so obvious to every good-natured and common-sensical person, what then goes wrong? Is every bad guest either half-witted or downright vicious – or both? Lord Chesterfield, in his old age – when his son had predeceased him and his godson (another Philip Stanhope) had become the equally unsatisfactory object of his instruction – thought otherwise. 'There are some who,' he told the godson in 1765, 'without the least visible taint of ill-nature or malevolence, seem to be totally indifferent, and do not show the least desire to please.' But 'whether this proceeds from a lazy, negligent, and listless disposition, from a gloomy and melancholy nature, from ill-health and low spirits, or from a secret and sullen pride, arising from the consciousness of their boasted liberty and independency' is, 'considering the various movements of the human heart, and the wonderful errors of the human mind ... hard to determine'.

Less indulgent towards the foibles of human hearts

and minds was the Reverend E.J. Hardy, Chaplain of Her Majesty's Forces and the author of a late nineteenth-century best-seller entitled *How To Be Happy Though Married*. (His authorship of this tract notwithstanding, the Reverend Mr. Hardy was chivalrous enough to think that women 'are as a rule better mannered than men'. That this should be so, he puts down to 'their greater sympathy and power of quicker intuition, [which] gives to them finer tact'.) 'Vanity, ill-nature, want of sympathy, want of sense,' he declared in *Manners Makyth Man* (1887), 'these are the chief sources from which bad manners spring. Nor can we imagine an incident in which a man could be at a loss as to what to say or do in company, if he was always considerate for the feelings of others, forgot himself and did not lose his head or leave his common sense at home.'

Consideration again.

Two

CALLING

'Let your visit be well tim'd ...'
– Adam Petrie, *The Rules of Good Deportment or Good Breeding* (date unknown)

'We are told,' says Lady Troubridge in *The Book of Etiquette* (1931), although she does not disclose by whom, 'that the origin of calling dates from the Stone Age, when the head of a family used to leave a roughly carved block of stone at the door (?) of another as a gesture of goodwill and friendship.' Be that as it may – and it almost certainly was not – by the mid-nineteenth century, the descendants of Lady Troubridge's stone-droppers had got the whole business of calling and the leaving of visiting cards down to a fine art. A bewildering mass of rules and conventions dictated who could or could not leave what sort of visiting card (though cards must be 'always engraved, *never* printed') on whom. And, just to make things more confusing for anyone with a taste for foreign travel, these conventions often varied from one country to another. For instance: 'According to the old-fashioned American custom, cards may be left by established members of the community at the house of any newcomer. In Latin countries the reverse is true: newcomers must be the first to leave the cards'. Or again: 'The upper right hand corner of the card is turned down with the point towards the name, to indicate that one has called in person – in most cases, a fiction of which nothing is left but the form. This custom is observed in Washington and in many foreign countries, but not in all. In Scandinavian capitals, for example, and in England, it only suggests that the cards have been mussed' (*Vogue's Book of Etiquette*, New York, 1948).

7

As a general rule, in their heyday, cards might be left at the house of anyone to whom a person had been introduced – although it had always to be remembered that 'a woman never calls on a man'. Certain calls were, however, obligatory. 'Calls of condolence, calls on the new mother, calls on out-of-town people who have entertained you in their home towns, calls on the fiancé of a relative, and calls on the bride and groom in their new home' – all of these were, in the opinion of Ethel Frey Cushing, inexorable social duties in America in the 1920s. Nor must you 'fail to leave a card, when calling', she goes on, 'for each member of the family who is of receiving age. A woman leaves one of her cards for each lady of the family and one of her husband's, and an extra one of her husband's for the man of the house'.

Mrs Humphry, alias 'Madge' of *Truth* magazine, was an expert on the more subtle purposes to which calls and visiting cards might be put. 'Cards must be left after an invitation,' she advises readers of *Manners for Men* (1887), 'whether the latter be accepted or not.' But 'in case of not wishing to pursue the acquaintance of the person who sent the invitation, it is sufficient to leave the cards without enquiring whether the lady of the house is at home'. In another case, 'If a man should wish, for any reason, to courteously end an acquaintanceship' (elsewhere 'Madge' devotes several pages to lamenting the decline of correct grammar), 'he can do it without any of the intolerable "cutting", a method resorted to only by the rough and unculti-vated. He may make a call that, in his own mind, he knows to be a final one, remaining only just the quarter of an hour that is the minimum length of such functions, and preserving a certain gravity of demeanour which is as free from "sulks" as it is from other forms of bad temper. After this, he may leave cards once more without asking if the ladies of the family are at home.'

Tedious and time-wasting as the performance of these rituals must have been, there is one enormous advantage of which the gradual disappearance of

8

these customs – and the rather less gradual disappearance of the armies of trained servants, on whom, of
course, the whole system depended – has deprived us.
For, if 'Madge's' gentleman was at liberty not to ask if
the lady was at home, the lady was no less free to have
a servant inform a would-be caller, that she was,
whatever the truth of the matter, 'not at home'. And
that, for at least that particular day, was that.

The Sultan's Adviser

London. February 1981. Outside, everything grey and
slushy: streets, sky, and buildings. Inside, lights on
everywhere, the gas furnace (she had telephoned the
Gas Board twice the week before and again yesterday
– 'We've got your name on the list, madam, but in
this weather, as you will appreciate ...'), the gas
furnace now switching itself off, now roaring into
ferocious and uncontrollable action. At this minute,
09.46 according to the digital clock on Henry's side of
the bed, the heat was, in its own dry way, as
unbearable as it had been on the hottest day of the
year she and Henry had spent in Bombay. Thanks to
the anti-burglar devices, which the Insurance Company had insisted that they must instal, the windows
would open no further than the few inches at the top
that she had already opened them. Nothing for it but
to go downstairs and fling wide the garden door,
which at least was still allowed to function as a door.
And then the washing...

The door-bell rang.

At 9.46? But, of course, it must be the man from
the Gas Board. She crossed to the window, pressed her
nose against the streaming glass.

Stepping backwards, a squat figure in what must
once have been a smart business man's overcoat came
into view. Whoever it was also sported a strange
wide-brimmed hat and was brandishing a very small
rose-bud on a very long stalk. But no tool box. Too
late, she recognised him; too late, she tried to shrink
back behind the curtains, out of sight.

9

'Why, there you are,' came the thick, plummy voice from below. 'Not a bad time, I hope? I thought I'd just call on you.'

'Shit,' said Maria Theresa. And then: 'Hell, why not?'

They had met him the night before, at dinner with friends. He was, he had said, at the moment the adviser to some Malaysian Sultan – it had sounded like Penang but wasn't quite that – on 'minerals'. No one had seemed sure what he meant by this but his stories of exotic places and happenings, while amusing enough, had sounded like pure fantasy. He had full, very pink, moist lips and tended to spit when he spoke. His name had struck her as so inappropriate that she had no difficulty in remembering it. She and

Henry had agreed on the way home that it was most unlikely that somebody with so Middle-Eastern a manner (Armenian perhaps?) could have started off life as Gilbert Howard.

'Come on in,' she said, kicking out behind her at a pile of dirty shorts and jerseys, trying to manoeuvre them into the kitchen. So that the sitting-room might overlook the garden, a previous owner had turned the house round: on occasions like this, coming straight through a small porch into a semi open-plan dining-room and kitchen had its drawbacks.

The rose was for her. He presented it with a solemn stoop of the head, although he didn't, as she rather expected him to do, kiss her hand.

'What a delightful place,' he said. 'Perfectly charming.'

'A bit of a mess today, I'm afraid. And the boiler's gone crazy. But, yes, we quite like it.'

In fact she was proud of the house, so proud that, if she had had the time to tidy things into their right places, she would have offered to show him round. In the two years since they had bought it, she had, slowly, room by room, done it over from top to bottom.

'That picture, though, the one over the fireplace, it should be six inches or so lower, of course. I could fix it for you easily.'

'Well, I don't know,' she said, taken aback. 'The thing is that all the good pictures are from Henry's family and he rather prides himself on knowing how to hang them.'

Gilbert did not appear to have heard her.

'At least six inches, probably more,' he said, advancing towards the fireplace, eyes narrowed, arms outstretched.

'What about some coffee?' she suggested, definitely alarmed now, and anxious to distract him. She would give him some coffee, that wouldn't take long. Then, with any luck, he would go and she could finish the children's washing, bake the cakes which she was supposed to deliver in the early afternoon.

11

Gilbert stopped in his tracks, hunched forward and sneezed a high-pitched sneeze. From his trouser pocket he pulled out a wad of crumpled tissues. Having examined it carefully, he detached a piece, blew his nose into it and, having inspected the result, put the ball of damp tissue into an ashtray.

Maria Theresa tried not to look at it.

'Coffee?' she suggested again.

'Never,' said Gilbert firmly. 'Most injurious to the system. But I'm interrupting you.' His eye had alighted, disapprovingly, on the heap of clothes at her feet.

'Oh no, not really,' she said feebly. 'Just the children's clothes and then I have to make sponges for a friend who runs a catering business.'

'Sponges?'

'Cakes.'

'Well, in that case,' said Gilbert, removing first gloves, then a muffler, then his overcoat, 'I wouldn't say no to a tisane. Camomile perhaps – or vervaine?'

'I don't think …'

'No tisanes?' He looked quite put out.

'Tea?'

'You have China tea?'

'Earl Grey, Oolong or Lapsong' – she felt ridiculously pleased with herself.

'Oolong,' said Gilbert. 'But just a hint. Very weak. With lemon. And you wouldn't happen to have a little cognac, would you? My chill, you know.'

Maria Theresa made the tea, fetched a glass and the brandy from the corner cupboard. Gilbert settled himself comfortably at the kitchen table, took out from his breast pocket a scruffy black notebook and a pen.

'You're from Texas, I believe,' he said.

'My mother and stepfather live there now,' she agreed. 'Until I was twelve, though, we lived mostly in Philadelphia.'

'I shall almost certainly be going to Texas soon on business,' Gilbert told her. 'Rather important business. Now where does your stepfather live?'

Miles from anywhere, she thought of saying. In the middle of the desert. But instead she said, quite truthfully, 'Houston.'

'Excellent. And his address, his telephone number?'

Again it crossed her mind to deceive him – she could always change a number or two: and again she didn't.

'Very comfortably off, your stepfather,' said Gilbert, returning his pen and notebook to his pocket. 'So I gather from our hosts of last night.'

'Oh no, not really,' she protested. 'And certainly not by Texas standards.'

Gilbert beamed at her. Another cognac, he said, would do the trick: but what trick she never discovered. An hour and a half and three cognacs later, he was still installed at the kitchen table. The temperature in the house was, he said, marvellous; it suited someone, who, like himself, was used to living in the tropics, just perfectly. After an hour or so of stories about the East – shark-fishing, man-eating tigers, she and Henry must, of course, come out there, as personal guests of the Sultan, he would see to it – she had tried to prod him on his way by emptying the washing machine and reloading it. He had carried on talking.

Now she said to him, with more than a touch, she hoped, of weariness in her voice: 'Well, I'd better be getting on with the cakes. They'll be late anyway.'

She stared hard at his overcoat and hat.

'Ah yes, cakes. What sort of cakes?'

She told him.

'I shall help you,' he said.

'Really, it isn't necessary. I mean,' she said, 'It's probably easier if I do it myself. I'm used to it.'

'Nonsense. I should be delighted. I've nothing else to do for a while.'

This was bad news.

Another shrill sneeze, another piece of tissue, another inspection, another scrumpled pellet – this time left on the kitchen table by the brandy bottle, which was empty. That, at least, was something. She had an idea. Opening and peering into a cupboard, she said, in what was supposed to be a surprised tone: 'Oh Hell, I'm clean out of chocolate.'

He might have offered to go for it. But he didn't.

'I'll hold the fort for you,' he said, instead. 'Look after things while you're gone.'

So it was she who went out to the grocery round the corner. If she hadn't known he would be waiting for her, she might well have enjoyed the change from the stifling atmosphere in the house, the icy trudge through the mushy streets.

'Is that you?' his voice rang out, as she pushed open the door of the porch. Across the dining room carpet there was creeping, from the direction of the kitchen, a crested surge of froth: the floor of the kitchen itself was awash with soapy water.

Gilbert stuck his head round the door frame. He had retreated on to the stairs.

'A most objectionable young man called,' he told her. 'From the Gas Board, he said, come to mend the boiler. I told him it was working perfectly well, as he could see for himself – and he couldn't have been more offensive. In any case, I got rid of him and I don't think he'll be back in a hurry.'

Not until that moment had she suspected him of outright malevolence.

'And this?' she pointed to the kitchen floor, to the sodden carpet. Could he have sabotaged the washing machine?

'Just a moment ago,' he said. 'But at least, since I managed to prevent that lout from tampering with your boiler, it should dry out quickly enough. And I found your chocolate for you. You must have been looking in the wrong place.'

So was that it? Had he rumbled her pathetic little ruse to get him out of the house, and decided to punish her for it? Well, it was her house, wasn't it, why shouldn't she ... but, evidently, in his view, no further explanations were necessary. Indeed, what was worse, in some extraordinary and infuriating way, he actually managed to make her feel cheap, even guilty.

14

'Probably best to start in the kitchen,' he said. 'When my bungalow flooded in Borneo, after the river had gone down again, the boys had everything back in order in no time.'

To Hell with your bungalow in Borneo, she thought, and with the boys too, as she set about swabbing the kitchen floor, emptying buckets, rolling back the dining room carpet.

When she had finished, Gilbert said, 'Well, better be getting on with those cakes then. If you're out of brandy, I wouldn't say no to a whisky.'

Prepared now to abandon his position of safety on the stairs, he picked his way over the rolled up carpet.

Meekly and feeling as pliable in his hands as one of his horrible tissues, she fetched the bottle.

Gilbert resumed his old position at the kitchen table, lifting up first one foot, then the other, to inspect the soles of his shoes.

'Can't be too careful with a chill,' he told her, and poured himself a large slug of whisky.

'While you were out,' he went on, after a thoughtful swig, 'I had a little look round the house. Some quite nice pictures you have in your sitting room – or at least they could be, if they were properly cleaned. As it happens, I have a little man …'

'Have you?' she heard herself say, rather sharply, as she dumped bowls, flour, butter on the table in front of him. Strangely, although she was for some reason unable to stand up for herself against this uninvited bully who had come to make her day a misery, although she had sat back and allowed him to flood her kitchen, send away the man from the Gas Board and very possibly ruin the dining room carpet, she was not prepared to listen to him criticizing the state of Henry's pictures. Encouraged by the new sharpness in her voice, she swept up the three or four balls of tissue that had accumulated beside him and banged them noisily into the trash can.

'It's odd you should think they need cleaning,' she said, gaining confidence. 'Because Henry has a cousin at Christies and the ones he thought needed doing were done only last year.'

'Really.' Gilbert's opinion of Christies, or at any rate of Henry's cousin, was clearly not a good one. 'And the Bokhara rug, too? I suppose it was Christies – or your husband's cousin – who recommended whoever it was who had a go at repairing that?'

And of course it had been. Maria Theresa contemplated the bag of flour she was holding. She would have liked to throw it at him, to see it explode in his face and all over him.

'Not that it's any of my business,' said Gilbert, as if to himself. 'Such a pity, though, to own perfectly reasonable things and then either to ruin them or to

16

refuse to show them off to proper advantage. But mind you, with those curtains...'

He was back on her ground and again she felt powerless to defend herself. So apparent was his belief in the infallibility of his own judgement that any form of protest was obviously doomed to failure. He would treat it, she knew, as no better than a childish display of temperament. How he had managed to force her into this corner, she had no idea: all she knew was that she must get him out of the house before he succeeded in getting her to make an idiot of herself. Without thinking what she was doing, she wiped the flour from her hands, washed them, and poured herself a Scotch.

If only somebody would telephone. Or could she say she must call about the cakes being late and get Claire to call her back? That way she could invent a sudden disaster. Or she could pretend to throw a fit. But she was such a bad liar, such a poor actress. And, whatever she did, would he go anyway? Unused to drinking neat whisky at any time, let alone on an empty stomach at a quarter to two in the afternoon (the one thing she was not going to do was to make any reference to its being lunch time, indeed rather past it), she knocked back her tot in one gulp.

17

Gilbert puckered his wet, rosy lips – with amusement, she supposed, and she was furious with herself. She knew what was coming.

It came.

'I thought you said you never drank in the day time?'

(He had, at quite an early point in the nightmare, offered her some of Henry's brandy.)

'Oh well, you know, in an – ' she stopped short.

If amused he had been in the first place, he was so no longer.

'In an emergency,' he said flatly, as he pulled himself up to his full height, puffing out his chest. At the same time his eyes became damp and spanielly.

'No, no, no…' he dismissed the words she had not yet found. 'There's no need to apologise. I can see that I have been a nuisance … in the way … a bore…'

'But of course you haven't.' Having, by a chance slip, achieved what she had hardly dared to hope for, it now seemed to her that, if she let him flounce out in a huff, all the effort she had put into controlling herself would somehow be wasted. 'Not in any way. I know what,' she said brightly, as he heaved himself into his coat. 'I was just going to suggest that I made us something to eat. Just a snack. I mean…'

'You have your cakes to make.' He pulled on his black leather gloves, arranged the muffler about his neck. 'And besides,' he said, 'I have an appointment.'

'Well, if you're sure…'

'Of course, I'm sure,' he said, quite unpleasantly. 'No, don't bother to see me out.'

Only now did she make a move to do so.

'If you're in this part of London again,' she started.

'I think it most unlikely,' he told her. 'But I'll give your love to your stepfather, tell your family how you are.'

And with this promise – or threat? – Gilbert Howard pulled his hat down firmly on to his head and disappeared through the front door.

When, later, Maria Theresa called her hostess of the previous evening, Sybil said, 'Oh my God, you

didn't tell him where you lived, did you? I had him
all day yesterday. You're lucky he's not still with you.'
Whether or not he was employed by any Sultan, he
had for the last three months, it appeared, been living
in a draughty bedsitter above a South London
pub – where, understandably, he liked to spend as
little time as possible. He was one of those people who
vanished for years on end and then, suddenly, popped
up again. 'He's got the hide of a hippopotamus,' said
Sybil. 'Or is it a rhinoceros? In any case, don't worry
too much, because it really does seem that he's
persuaded some North African consortium that he's
an expert in something and he's off to the States any
minute. I've even seen his ticket. To Houston, I think.
Perhaps it's oil?'

Dropping In

'Do drop in any time you're passing' is a phrase which
many people use to avoid issuing any more specific
invitation. It is sometimes meant, more often not
meant. The best way to discover which is the case is to
telephone before presenting yourself on the doorstep.

Droppers-in may have some ulterior motive – as
Gilbert Howard very probably had – but, as a rule,
they merely have time to kill, which they find it dull
to do alone. How much more amusing, the reasoning
goes, to spend the morning drinking endless cups of
coffee, or the afternoon polishing off a bottle of vodka,
in company. After all, is what the intended companion thinks he has to do really so vital?

Especially vulnerable to droppers-in are housewives, who spend much of their time at home, and
people whose occupations do not take them away to
some official place of work. So he's a sculptor, so she's
a novelist ('bohemians' these, very possibly, to whom
any thought of regular hours must surely be anathe-
ma), so all she's got to do is to cook the children's
lunch or sweep out the larder – let's brighten up their
day (or night) by dropping in on them. But, oddly
enough, there are a lot of people who need time to

19

themselves, whether for work or, quite simply, to relax. And if such people did want to see the dropper-in, couldn't they telephone to invite him, her or them (some droppers-in prefer to operate in groups) to come round?

In general, the dropper-in is more certain of a warm welcome in rural areas or where there is plenty of space, less certain in a city or where the person dropped-in on lives in a cramped apartment. But, just as there are people who crave solitude, so there are others who delight in the stimulus of noise and other human beings constantly around them. To such a person even the Sultan's adviser may well appear as a boon.

Curiously, it seems to be a fairly common assumption that anybody else's nature – unless that other person be either a misanthrope or a psychiatric case – must be much the same as one's own. Otherwise, nobody would have thought it necessary to point out that the first and most important task of any guest (whether an unscheduled dropper-in or a weekend guest invited several weeks before the event) is to try to gauge the characters of his or her hosts – and, in so doing, to pay particular attention to the ways in which these may differ from his or her own. 'Because,' as Lord Chesterfield put it, 'the same thing that would be civil at one time, and to one person, may be quite otherwise at another time, and to another person.' Or again: 'Remember that there is a local propriety to be observed in all companies; and that what is extremely proper in one company, may be and often is, highly improper in another.'

Three

PARTIES

'One knows the very nature of both man and woman by their actions at table. One suddenly sees their innermost characters, their attitudes, their breeding, but above all, one knows whether one wants to spend another evening at table with them.' A nineteenth-century Bostonian, quoted in *The Amy Vanderbilt Complete Book of Etiquette,* revised and expanded by Letitia Baldridge (1978).

'Good manners socially are not unlike swimming – not the 'crawl', or 'overhand', but smooth, tranquil swimming.' *Emily Post's Etiquette* (1922).

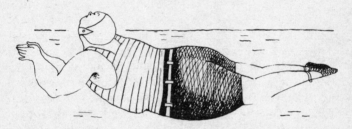

'Entertaining should be a simple matter,' wrote Millicent Fenwick, in *Vogue's Book of Etiquette,* 'and, in prehistoric times, perhaps it was. One liked someone, one asked him to come and share whatever game had been caught, and that was the end of it. But this happily logical state of affairs can't have lasted long, if it ever really existed at all. Even in biblical times, a philosophy and a ritual for entertaining had already crept into the picture, and they have stayed ever since.'

The 'ritual of entertaining' – and, still more, of being entertained – is the stuff of Etiquette Books: how to behave, what to wear, what to say or what not to say, when presented to the Queen of England, when asked to dinner at the White House, to a

diplomatic function or an official banquet, and so on, down the scale, to 'five o'clock tea'; at which, in 1898, according to Mrs Humphry's *Manners for Men,* 'gentlemen' were 'in great request' and their 'duties ... rather onerous'. 'They have to carry teacups about, hand sugar, cream and cakes or muffins, and keep up all the time a stream of small talk, as amusing as they can make it. They must rise every time a lady enters or leaves the room, opening the door for her exit if no one else is nearer to do it, and, if the hostess requests it, they must see the lady downstairs to her carriage or cab.'

Nor was this all. 'With regard to the viands, a man helps himself, but not till he has seen that all the ladies in the vicinity have everything they can possibly want. His hostess, or some lady deputed by her to preside over the tea-table, gives him tea or coffee, and he adds cream and sugar.'

Inevitably (and, in most people's view, fortunately), things are rather simpler today. But those three basic characteristics, to which Millicent Fenwick attributes the desire to entertain, are still with us. Perhaps never more so. These are 'a human feeling of friendliness, which we like to think of as natural to man'; 'a conception, perhaps nomadic in origin, of the obligation of hospitality'; and 'the Old Testament obligation of honouring the guest'. So all kinds of parties continue to be given by all sorts of people. At a recent Californian party (filmed by a television company), the host was a chow-chow dog. His guests, other

canines, some of long and some of shorter pedigree, sat up to plates of jelly, cake and chocolate, all wearing frocks or suits (according to sex) and neat bibs and tuckers. In the middle of the meal, the singing-telegram man arrived with a singing-telegram. The owners of the host and guests were delighted. After the party, the commentator reported, over half the guests threw up.

Anything and everything can be – and often is – the occasion for all kinds of junketing. But, returning to the more usual sort of parties, to which human beings invite others of their own species, the majority of writers on etiquette and entertaining agree that of cocktail parties, dinner parties and dances, most relaxing and satisfying is the dinner party, which is given in somebody's house or apartment and at which the number of diners is somewhere between that of the evangelists and that of the apostles (i.e. between four and twelve).

Dick and Marcella

Alice was adamant. She had asked them for eight o'clock. Because she always asked people for eight o'clock, didn't she? And hadn't Lester and Arlene arrived just after eight? And Ron and Lenore just after them? What was more, she had sent them a card to confirm the date, a card on which she had given them not only your address but, in case they should have to cancel – which was what she very much hoped they might do – the telephone number. She didn't altogether trust her sister's judgement; still less her brother-in-law's. Just because they had been on a cruise and had met a couple who happened to live in your city, why should you want to ask these people to dinner? But then Sandy (Alice's sister) had been so keen on the whole thing, so insistent. 'Why not ask Lester and Arlene and Ron and Lenore,' you had said. 'That way there'll be eight of us and, if they're as awful as you think they're going to be, at least the rest of us can have a good time.'

Once you got used to the idea, you had even begun quite to look forward to the evening. After all, they might not be that bad. According to Sandy, the guy – Dick was his name, that was it – kept an ocean-going boat in the bay. He was thinking of getting it taken round to the Caribbean. Hence the cruise. To check out the area. Well, why shouldn't you and Alice…?

But here you and your friends are, and here Dick and his wife are not, at nine o'clock, with everyone hungry, nobody wanting yet another drink and Alice mad at you for having persuaded her to wait dinner a minute after a quarter of nine. 'It may not be a soufflé,' she is saying now to Lenore. 'But it is a roast en croûte, which can't go on cooking a second longer. Or do we want soggy pastry and cold meat, along with a hot sauce and vegetables?'

24

Alice, you have to admit, has a point. Her food is good. She takes trouble. And how much longer, anyway, can you go on saying that, if you are having her sister's friends to dinner, then you might as well make it as pleasant for them as possible? Very probably Alice has been right all along and they have forgotten. Or decided to chuck. So, after one more call to Dick and Marcella's house – again no reply –– you all go into the dining room.

Having cleared away the two extra places, the six of you sit down. The spicy mayonnaise in which Alice has tossed the lobster salad is terrific, everyone says, even for Alice; the wine too (your department) is perfect; Alice, you see, is herself again, relaxed and not a hint of crankiness, as she takes the empty bowls into the kitchen, returns with her beef dish. She is on her way back to the kitchen when Arlene is interrupted in mid-anecdote by the ringing of the front door bell, immediately followed by loud knocking.

'Christ,' everyone hears Alice scream. 'I just don't believe it.'

'You could always tell them we've finished,' Lester suggests.

Not a bad idea, you think. But, 'No, come on everybody,' you say. 'Let's make it look like we were expecting them.' As you go off to answer the door, your friends begin hastily resetting the table.

'Hi,' says a thickly-built, florid man, with a self-confident paunch, brightly checked trousers and a differently checked jacket. 'Dick Trapp. And this,' he pushes forward a woman of perhaps forty, with a spoilt mouth and fluffy blonde hair, 'is my Marcella. The better half, as some people say, ha ha!'

And, so far as appearances go, at any rate, you wouldn't argue with those people.

'Hi,' says Marcella, in a small, whiny voice. 'I really am sorry...'

'Not good, eh?' Dick punches you playfully in the stomach. 'That's the trouble with these goddam drinks parties. And, you know what they're like, now the little girl needs the john.'

You peer into the darkness. Has the little girl eaten, you wonder? Will she sleep in the car? Or need a room? But the little girl is Marcella.

'Just show her where it is and leave her to it,' says Dick, again shoving his wife in front of him. 'She'll follow her nose when she's through. Won't you, little girl?'

'Sure,' says Marcella, and thanks you for showing her the bathroom. 'I'll be right along.'

'Great,' says Dick and, when you usher him into the dining room, where everything has been rearranged and everyone, including Alice, is in their new seats: 'Hi, folks and humble apologies. But you know what these drinks parties are. And then the route here. Dick Trapp. With two ps. Hahaha!'

Only now do you see that your four guests have been served with the beef, which they have already started to eat.

'I thought they'd better go on,' says Alice, noticing you noticing this. As she gets up to welcome Dick, her face manages to assume two very different expressions simultaneously: one the official friendly smile of the hostess, the other (can it be her eyes?) definitely hostile.

'I'm so glad you could come,' she says in a neutral voice.

'Really glad to be invited,' says Dick, insisting on shaking, not only Alice's hand, but those of your other guests too.

'And Marcella?' Alice asks, as Dick does his round of the table.

'In the john. Even thoroughbreds have to do it, haha! And she sure is some thoroughbred, my Marcella, I can tell you.'

Lenore catches your eye.

'Sure is,' says Dick, with a burp. 'One too many martinis, I guess, haha! Here she is. My little girl.'

Those who have to turn round in their chairs to take a look at this phenomenon.

'Oh my,' says Marcella. 'We really are late, aren't we? I'm so …'

27

'Not at all,' says Alice. 'But after we'd called you a couple of times, we thought you must have forgotten.' Untrue to usual form, she seems to be prepared to forgive the wife sooner than the husband. Having introduced Marcella to the others, she points to Marcella's place, on your right, and to Dick's, on her own right. 'Now, I'll just get you some lobster salad – that is, of course, if you can eat …'

'Sure can,' says Dick, smacking his lips. 'Why, you guys certainly …'

'No, no, don't do that,' says Marcella. 'We're so late, why don't we just join in with whatever you're all …'

'What and miss the lobster?' Dick interrupts her. 'Not on your life, little girl. Just because you got the vomits in Mystic? Oh no.'

'But Dick, dear …'

'Not on your life. Dick Trapp likes his lobster and he's going to have it. Aren't I right?'

He looks round the table, as if asking for confirmation. Lenore makes a strange mewing sound. But that is all.

'Well, not for me, anyway,' says Marcella.

'Guess it must have been a hen lobster she got,' says Dick, elbowing Arlene, on his right, in the ribs. 'Did you know a female lobster was called a "hen"? What do you suppose tthat makes the male of the species, eh?'

'A cock?' suggests Arlene.

Dick is delighted. 'Do you hear that, everyone?' he roars, shaking with a mirth which he clearly believes to be infectious. 'And who's her poor husband? This cute little lady on my right doesn't know the difference between a lobster and a cock.'

Lester, the poor husband in question, tries to force a smile.

'Great tits, though,' says Dick.

Alice, coming back into the room with his lobster, looks startled.

It wouldn't have surprised you if, there and then, Dick had plunged his pudgy fist straight into Arlene's cleavage. But he doesn't.

28

'Did you ever see anything so good?' he asks instead, taking the bowl from Alice and showing it round, tipped sideways, for everyone to see. A couple of chunks of lobster fall out on to his place mat, another on to the floor.

'Ah well. Every cloud, I guess,' says Dick, as he lowers his head into Arlene's lap. Having retrieved first the piece of lobster from the floor ('Great thighs, too!'), then the other two from his place mat, he thrusts all three into his mouth, with his fingers.

'Hmmm. Sure are some cook,' he says, masticating appreciatively, to Alice. 'This turnip you've got in here?'

'No,' says Alice. 'It's celeriac. Root celery.'

'Well, I'd hate to argue with you.' With a gulp, he swallows what is in his mouth, then picks up his fork. 'But I'd still take a bet on it. Sure I would. Turnip.' In goes a heaped forkful. 'Because my old Dad, you see, he had this plot. Knew everything there is to know about vegetables, he did. And I used to help him.' Another gulp, another forkful. 'Yes, we were poor, I don't mind admitting it.' (What's this got to do with anything?) 'Not like the little girl over there, of course. She has class. As you can see.' A piece of lobster – or celeriac? – shoots out of his mouth, lands on Arlene's cheek. After a pause, she picks it off. 'No, we were poor folk. Shit poor. But hard-working. That's how I got where I am today. And what's the matter with that, I'd like to know?'

He surveys the assembled company. Nobody says anything.

'Well, I'm not complaining, anyway,' says Dick, scratching together the last morsels of salad and loading them into his mouth. 'What's this? Two kinds of wine? Smart stuff, eh, little girl? But Scotch and soda for Dick Trapp,' he says, looking at you. 'That's if you don't mind, naturally.'

While Alice clears away Dick's salad bowl, serves the Trapps and yourselves with beef, you go off to get the whisky. On your return, you find Dick sniffing at the sauce boat.

29

'Morilles,' Alice is explaining. 'A sort of mushroom. Even when they've been dried they're supposed to have more flavour.'

'More flavour, eh? Well, that's all right by me.' Dick fishes out from the sauce boat as many of the black mushrooms as he can find. 'Clever girl,' he tells Alice.

Arlene passes you what remains of the sauce.

'Jesus!' With something between a sneeze and a hiccough, Dick spits a couple of partly chewed morilles out on to his plate. 'You sure these goddam fungus aren't poisonous?'

'Dick,' says Marcella reprovingly.

Dick is suddenly the small boy. 'Well, hell, Marcie, I mean I've never had these things before, have I? How was I to know?'

'Even so …'

'Alice was telling us,' says Lenore, coming to the rescue, 'that you have a boat in the bay.'

'Sure do,' says Dick, carefully scraping the rest of the sauce off his beef, then helping himself to a large dollop of butter and smearing that over his meat instead. 'And a very beautiful boat it is. Decor's the little girl's department, of course. Pretty classy. As you can imagine. And she's got great engines, too. Perkins. Last year we got her down to …'

As Dick settles in to a detailed account of life aboard the *Richella* – 'Richard and Marcella, get it? Marchard sounded kind of dumb to us' – you feel you should start up a conversation with Marcella. Does she enjoy these boat trips, you wonder?

She shakes her head. 'I get sick.' And that is not her only problem, you soon discover. Too much sun is not good for her kind of colouring. She gets migraines. Some of her friends have been cured by acupuncture. But she can't bear the thought of those needles. She has trouble eating. (She has, you notice, eaten practically nothing; just a few vegetables.) Sleeping, too, is difficult. Even with pills, she wakes up in the early hours and can't get back to sleep again. Dick is such a help normally, he's so positive, but Dick (no surprise) is a heavy sleeper. She supposes that he must be right, that she's highly strung, very sensitive. You don't have children? Well, she has. Three. The eldest, a boy, is at college now. He was so cute when he was a baby. But, of course, you mustn't have favourites. He's a good boy though. All her kids are good. (You are shown photographs.) And nice-looking too, don't you think? But still a mother can't help worrying. Are they really telling you everything? And all those drugs. And the perverts. It's so difficult these days.

All you have to do is to nod sympathetically. Thoroughly depressed by now, you have seen both Ron and Lenore and Alice and Lester trying to talk to one another. Impossible. The beef was finished long ago, the dessert has been and gone, you have poured wine and whisky, Alice is in the kitchen making the coffee and still Dick is pumping out the nautical exploits.

'Hell,' he is shouting, 'the guy may have been a yid,' (Ron is a 'Yid': does Dick know? if he did, would he care?) 'but he certainly didn't ask for kosher wine or any of that piss. No sir. He sat up on the bridge there with the rest of us and we knocked off three quart bottles between the five of us. Not bad, eh?'

As Alice comes in with coffee, Dick, with a hearty guffaw, leans back in his chair, tipping it away from the table. There is a sharp splintering sound.

'Shit,' says Dick, jumping up. 'I guess I've broken the goddam thing.'

'I'm always telling you, dear,' says Marcella.

'I know, little girl. And I'm sorry. But least said, soonest mended, eh? Just get it fixed,' he tells Alice, 'and send me the bill.'

Uncertain as to how Alice will take this, you say quickly: 'Don't worry. It's not the first time.'

This is untrue.

'Why,' says Alice, eyeing the broken chair, 'don't we have our coffee in the other room?'

'Great idea,' says Dick, who has nowhere to sit now. 'But hold it. Just a moment. Any of you guys know the one about the special commercial for the deaf?'

Unfortunately, none of you does.

'But Dick, dear,' Marcella protests.

'Well, it's like this, you see. There's this commercial they want to put over for the deaf, so they get in a guy who can do deaf and dumb language. Signs and that. Well, they get the cameras rolling – everyone watching me? – they get the cameras rolling and the guy starts off: "Good evening, ladies." ' Over his own ample breasts, Dick clamps his cupped hands. 'Get it? "Ladies." Hahaha. "Cut," shouts the director. "This is American television. We can't put out filth like that." "But this is deaf and dumb language," the guy explains. "Okay? That's how you say ladies." "Looks kind of awful to me," says the director. "But okay, let it roll." And the guy starts off again, from the top. "Good evening, ladies" ' (same gesture) ' "and gentlemen" ' (Dick grabs betwccn his legs at his chequered trousers.) 'Get it? "Gentlemen". "Cut," yells the director. "But this is deaf and dumb talk," the guy tells him. The director can't believe it. But, "Okay, just get on with it," he says. "Right," says the guy. And they roll it. "Good evening, ladies" ' (again Dick shakes his mammary glands), ' "and gentlemen" ' (again he clutches at his groin – but, this time, he seems to have discovered something and, yes, there he is, suddenly, pretending to beat himself off), ' "it gives me great pleasure …" Get it? "It gives me great pleasure …' Oh ho, hahaha!'

Told by anyone else, it might perhaps have been funny.

'It gives me great pleasure,' Dick says over and over again, the sweat pouring down his face, as he jerks his hand wildly up and down in front of Arlene's nose. 'It gives me great pleasure. Hahahaha!'

'It certainly seems to,' you hear Alice say to Ron, not at all under her breath.

'Dick just loves to tell stories,' says Marcella.

'Hey, anyone know the one about the girl who gets the obscene call?' Dick asks, having got his breath back. But this time people are quicker off the mark. Everyone follows Alice, with the coffee, into the sitting room. You, who have waited till the others are out of the room, are taken firmly by the sleeve and told the one about the girl who got the obscene call.

'Not bad, eh?' Dick splutters beside you, again repeating the punch line. 'If you can hold it in one hand, forget it! Not bad, eh?'

From then on, the course of the evening is set. Alice serves the coffee, you pour out drinks and more drinks, put on records. In the space of a few hours, you have learned more about the problems of motherhood (Arlene and Lenore, too, have children, but it seems that their lives are somehow easier than Marcella's is) and heard more 'stories' than you would have thought possible. At about 11.30 Marcella feels she may have a migraine coming on and tells Dick that she thinks they ought to go home. But Dick will have none of it. 'Shit, Marcie, the evening's just beginning to get going. Why not take some of your pills?' But they are a perfect couple, all the same. He is where he is because he worked for it. Yes sir. And she has class. Yes sir. This is America, isn't it? Yes sir. 'It gives me great pleasure, hahahaha!'

By one o'clock, your other guests, who have loyally tried to see you through the ordeal, can bear it no longer.

'Work tomorrow,' says Lester.

'Me too,' says Ron.

'And don't I have to work?' With a snort, Dick pulls himself to his feet, lurches sideways and smacks his glass down on the table. 'Still, you're all great guys. Better have them over to our place soon, eh, little girl?' To prevent himself from keeling over, he grabs hold of Lester. 'In fact I'd ask you all over there now, if you had a bit more goddam stamina.'

Lester, then Ron, are thumped on the back. Lenore succeeds in avoiding a wet kiss on the lips, but Arlene is less skilful. Surreptitiously, she wipes Dick's saliva off her face with the back of her hand.

Alice shudders.

'We'll be back in a minute,' you tell Marcella.

'Looks like you've got him for the night,' says

Lenore on the doorstep. And this is indeed what it looks like; when you and Alice get back into the sitting room, you find Marcella mopping up Dick's overturned whisky and Dick himself laid out full-length, with his feet up, on the sofa.

'I've never known him so bad,' Marcella whimpers, tears starting to her eyes.

'Oh no?' says Alice.

'And I can't drive. He's never passed out on me before. Never. Do you think he's had a coronary? Oh my God.'

'It'll wear off,' you say. 'You could both of you stay here the night.'

'Oh no, we couldn't do that. I mean I don't have my pills.'

'It's too late to try to get a cab out here.'

'Oh, I know it is, I know it is.' Suddenly Marcella seems to fold in half and, slumping into a chair, with her head between her hands, begins to sob. 'We should have gone ... we should have gone when my migraine started to come on.'

'If we take them home,' Alice hisses in your ear, 'at least they wont be here in the morning. Imagine breakfast.'

'He'll still have to come back for his car.'

'Even so.'

The thought of breakfast together decides you. 'Okay, I'll do it,' you say. 'No point in us both going though. Just help me get him to the car.'

Somehow you manage to heave Dick on to your shoulder and, with Alice and the still snivelling Marcella supporting him under his other armpit, drag him across the sitting room and on through the hall. In the driveway, he belches, seems to wake up for a moment, says 'Shit' and goes slack again. As soon as you get him into the back of your car, he begins to snore. Luckily (since Marcella has no idea which way they came) you know their part of the city quite well. Forty-five minutes later you are back home. Alice has cleared up and is in bed, waiting for you.

34

'Fixed up the dates then, for the Caribbean trip, have you?' she asks.

'We leave a month Saturday. Just the four of us,' you tell her. 'So that we can get to know each other better.'

'I've a good mind to ring Sandy right now,' says Alice. 'I feel like waking her and her idiot husband up in the middle of the night and bawling at them.'

Four

OUT ON THE TOWN

'Narrowed down to one sentence, a guest's manners should express, "I know you have tried to please me, and I am touched and made happy by that; but most of all I want you to know that all the ways in which you have planned to please me have been most successful." '
- Millicent Fenwick, *Vogue's Book of Etiquette*, 1948.
'The basic principles of conduct at any public entertainment are the same: Do not draw attention to yourself by noisy or conspicuous behaviour.'
- *The New Emily Post's Etiquette*, Elizabeth L. Post, 1975.

George and Christina

March 28: Max and Annabel are married. Instead of a honeymoon (of which, in all but name, they have already had several), they put in two weeks' hard labour on the garden of the small, as yet unmodernised, terraced house, which the combination of a mortgage and a generous contribution from Annabel's father have made it possible for them to buy.

May 4: Max, who first went into publishing eight years ago, only a few weeks after leaving university, starts a new job at Arnold Pinkney, a firm now run by the late Sir Arnold's son George (aged sixty-eight, according to *Who's Who*). At the end of this, his first day, George Pinkney suggests that Max and his wife come to dinner 'at the house' on May 21. 'Very kind of you.' 'Not at all, dear boy. My wife will give your wife the details.'

May 5: Christina Pinkney rings Annabel. 'Eight-thirty for nine. Just a few friends. Informal, naturally.'

May 21: Max and Annabel, having been admitted to the Pinkneys' bamboo and *trompe l'oeil* Chinese hall-way, are ushered in to meet their hostess. Christina, whose mother (everyone knows) is a celebrated set designer, is taller and rather younger than Gerge, to whom she has been married for about five years. Not that she hasn't been married before. To be numbered among her ex-husbands are a well-known critic (dead, alas, of drink) and a not so well-known painter (still extant).

As the opulently furnished yet oddly uncomfortable drawing room begins to fill up, it soon becomes clear that the Pinkneys (or at least one of them – Max feels certain that most of the guests must be Christina's friends) have a predilection for 'names'; of the twenty or so other people, there are only four of whom Max has not heard; and of these the Oriental turns out to be not only a Thai prince but a 'brilliant illustrator', and the aggressive little man with wiry hair a Professor of Biology.

No less noticeable is the fact that George Pinkney, who seldom has a cigar far from his lips, does not expect his wife to scrimp. Lavishness is everywhere in evidence: in the two immaculate waiters who serve drinks and who later wait at table; in the mass of lilies; in the food; in the wines; in the huge display of liqueurs and white alcohols. Even if some of the guests do (as Max and Annabel do) find the atmos-phere strangely unconvivial, almost chilly, only the most pampered of them could have said afterwards that they had not been exposed to the very best that money (George) and 'taste' (Christina – or, perhaps, some smart decorator?) could provide.

May 22: Max has a hangover and is late for work. Nobody seems to mind. In the afternoon, George tells him how much he enjoyed meeting Annabel. 'Such an unaffected girl. And so bright. She made a great hit, too, with Christina.' Deep draw on cigar. 'Which isn't always the case, I can assure you, dear boy.'

This heartening piece of news notwithstanding,

Max and Annabel spend the evening wondering how they can ever hope adequately to repay, as custom (and indeed interest) demand they should, the Pinkneys' munificent hospitality? In the first place their house is a shambles. Phase one of the modernisation, the demolition work, has been completed on schedule. But, despite repeated telephone calls and the promises that these have elicited, the builders seem curiously reluctant to embark on Phase two: construction. The demolition work having turned their newly planted garden into a heap of rubble, even a Sunday barbecue – which it is in any case most improbable that either George or Christina would enjoy – is out of the question. So what about a small dinner in a restaurant, with a few friends? Unfortunately, though, Max is not at all clear whether the singularity of Christina's taking to Annabel is due to Mrs Pinkney's not caring, as a rule, for younger women or because she likes her friends to have 'names'? Older people, then? Play it safe. But names? Annabel's parents, perhaps? Retired admirals, though no rarity, are still not exactly two-a-penny; and perhaps Christina might reveal a hitherto unsuspected passion for old-fashioned roses? Most unlikely. Indeed, on reflection, it has to be recognised that between The Old Water Mill and the Palais Pinkney there exists a great and, almost certainly, unbridgeable gulf.

So ... what to do?

May 22 – June 23: At least three times a week, and usually more often, the problem is brought out, discussed at length and abandoned, each time seemingly more impossible of solution. In early June, the builders deliver lengths of fibre-glass cornice and timber, bags of cement and plaster: and vanish again.

June 23: Max tells Annabel that he has heard the Pinkneys are leaving in mid-July to spend a month in Greece. They may even stay away another fortnight, which would bring them to September. Something must be done. And soon.

June 24: 3 a.m. Annabel wakes Max. Doesn't Christina 'adore' the theatre? Isn't George a great gourmet? So why don't they take them to the theatre – the Pinkneys might even choose the play – and afterwards, out to a really good dinner? Since the play will take up the first half of the evening, it could just be the four of them, and that will preclude them from having to try to produce 'suitable' friends.

'I think you've got it. I really do,' says Max. 'But don't ring her before eleven. Not even her best friends, apparently, dare to do that.'

11 a.m. Annabel calls Christina, hopes she hasn't woken her? 'What, at eleven?' Christina sounds quite put out. 'I'm up at seven every day. It's the only time I can get any work done.' Annabel's suggestion, nevertheless, is a 'sweet' one. As it happens, Christina has a friend opening in a new play next week. That would be 'heaven'. The only problem will be finding a day. She'll just get her diary ... 'No, no, no no ... ah, yes now, it'll have to be the week after that, what about Monday the 13th? Not superstitious, are you?' No, Annabel is not superstitious. The 13th will do fine. She'll let Christina know what time the play starts. It will be easiest, they both agree, to meet at the theatre. 'And we thought we might go on afterwards to Le Nid du Duc.' 'Le Nid du Duc? One of my very favourites. What heaven!'

July 13: 7.15 p.m. Max and Annabel are in the front lobby of the theatre at the agreed time.

7.25 p.m. Out of a taxi steps the lanky frame of the second Mrs Pinkney, arrayed in a scarlet and gold harem outfit, and with her hair teased into a profusion of dangling Pre-Raphaelite curls. But no sign of George. 'Oh, there you are,' Christina cries, spotting Max. 'Isn't it awful, I was in such a rush I've come out without any money. Could you be an angel?' Max is an angel and pays off her cab.

Would she like a quick drink? Or perhaps it's too late?

'Oh no, it's extraordinary, I know, but even with a

39

mother in the business, I still have to go straight in there and soak up the atmosphere. Why, Harriet!'

'Christina!'

Max and Annabel stand by as Christina and Harriet peck each other on the cheek, agree that they must have lunch together the moment Christina gets back from 'the islands'.

The two minute bell rings.

'Till September, then,' Christina tells Harriet and, turning to Max and Annabel, says breathlessly: 'Such a wonderful friend, Harriet. And so *talented*. You'd better leave George's ticket at the box-office. They'll see that he gets it.'

George, it appears, has had to go to a committee meeting. Somehow, he and Christina must have got their wires crossed. But then George doesn't really care much for the theatre in any case. He'll come on as soon as he can. All this Christina explains over her shoulder, as the house lights begin to dim and they are hurried down the aisle. With little help from the flickering beam of the usherette's torch, they push their way past people into the centre of the seventh row of the stalls.

The curtain rises and there is light. Christina leans forward, taps the man in front of her on the shoulder.

'Lazzaro!'

The man turns round.

'Christina!'

'Sh!'

'Sh!'

'Just my luck,' says a male voice from behind Christina, 'to have to sit behind a bloody bird's nest like that.'

'Tell her to sit back then,' a woman's voice replies. 'If you don't want to, I will.'

'No, I will.'

'Sh!'

'See you later,' Christina tells Lazzaro.

'Would you mind sitting back, Madam?'

'Sh!'

Christina sits back.

'Doesn't make any bloody difference anyway.'

'We could change seats?'

'And what would you see?'

'Well, I don't mind. It's just … '

'Sh!'

'Bloody woman with her bloody wig!'

Now Christina is sitting forward again, clapping, clapping. Her friend has made his first entrance.

'Darling Toots,' she says to Max. 'But the set. Isn't it awful!'

'Sh!'

As the first of the two acts unfolds, it is soon made plain, not only to Max and Annabel, but to everybody else in their vicinity, that darling Toots (whose name, so far as the general public is concerned, is David) should never have agreed to appear in such an 'amateurish', in such an 'unbelievably *insensitive*' production. Although there is still a certain amount of shushing – especially when Christina shouts 'Bravo, bravo!' on one of Toots's exit lines – the man in whose way she is seems to have fallen asleep. Not till the end of the act does he wake up again.

'And what's the bloody woman doing now?' he wants to know.

'It's the interval, dear.'

To Max, the play so far has seemed, if not strikingly original, at least a workmanlike piece of theatre, which will probably run for some time. Annabel, if anyone had asked her opinion, would have gone further: the only thing that is spoiling the play for her is Christina's non-stop commentary on it.

'A disgrace,' Christina tells Lazzaro, in front of her. 'If it weren't for Toots, I'd have got up and left after five minutes. Out of loyalty, though, I suppose I shall have to stay to the bitter end – and then go round to commiserate with the poor darling.'

'You really think it that bad?'

Most emphatically, Christina does; and so she stops in the middle of the aisle, effectively blocking it, to tell a friend she sees on the way out to the bar. Max has ordered a bottle of champagne to be ready for them. But Christina doesn't drink champagne

'except, very occasionally, at weddings'. A Campari and soda is what she would like, 'with masses of ice'.

As Max fights his way through to the bar, Annabel shifts from one foot to the other, listening to Christina telling one person after another – can there be many people in the place she doesn't know – how appalling it is that an actor of darling Toots's calibre should be treated in this way. Have they ever seen such an ill-cast, such a 'thoroughly Heath Robinson' production? The play itself? Well, without Toots of course it would be nothing. And the set? 'This Plowden man's supposed to be so wonderful, isn't he? I can't wait to ring Mummy in Los Angeles.'

The five minute bell has already rung when Max returns with Christina's Campari.

'Thank you, darling,' says Mrs Pinkney, taking the glass. To Annabel's surprise, she remembers to introduce her as well as Max to the old man in a threadbare velvet jacket, with whom she has been for the last few minutes in deep conversation. 'He works for George,' she adds, gesturing vaguely in Max's direction. 'They're very pleased with him' and turns her back again.

At the sound of the two minute bell, the old man is duly kissed on both cheeks and shuffles off towards the auditorium. Christina takes a quick sip of her Campari and puts it down on the shelf running round the edge of the bar, beside the scarcely touched bottle of champagne.

'Here we go again,' she says. 'Like lambs to the slaughter.'

Back in their places, Christina remains standing up, scanning the rows behind her. There is Harriet again. And there, apparently, is another friend. And another. Having waved at them all, blown the last one a kiss, Christina sits down.

The second act is no more to her liking than the first. By the time George stumbles across Annabel's legs, at about twenty to ten, Mrs Pinkney is beside herself. 'Words can't describe it,' she tells her husband. 'It's simply terrible.'

'Really?' George doesn't sound too interested. 'Sorry to be so late, old boy,' he leans across Christina to tell Max. 'An important committee meeting.'

'Sh!'

Having by his arrival woken up the man behind Christina ('What's going on?'), George settles comfortably into his seat and is, in no time at all himself asleep. Annabel is delighted at the interposition of this barrier between herself and the outraged Christina. Unlike Max, she is able to give her uninterrupted attention to the last forty minutes of what, despite Christina's strictures, she finds to be an absorbing, indeed very moving situation.

'How can they?' says Christina indignantly, as the curtain falls to enthusiastic applause. 'Don't they know proper theatre from rubbish?'

'What's that?' asks George, with a yawn, rubbing the bridge of his nose.

'Can this be the sort of rubbish,' Christina says, 'the theatre-going public actually wants?'

'Very likely,' George thinks.

'Then they should be re-educated. And fast. I've simply got to go round. How Toots must need cheering up!'

'They seem to be clapping loudly enough.'

'Because they don't know any better.'

'He could have said no. Probably needed the money. In any case, I'm for dinner. These committees take it out of you.' He winks at Max. 'No point in arguing with *her* though.'

Max wonders if he should wait for Christina? No, she'll join them later.

In the cab, on the way to the restaurant, George lights up a cigar and, between long puffs on it, treats Max and Annabel to a blow by blow account of his performance at this evening's session of The Committee for the Revitalization of the British Film Industry: the trouble is, of course, there are too many Union officials on the Committee; the sort of chaps who'd cut off their noses to spite their faces; nevertheless, George thinks he has managed to knock some sense

44

into them; even that kind of chap has to see in the end that Americans aren't going to pour money down too obvious a drain; the Minister, who is with George one hundred per cent – but, of course, mustn't show it – was very gratified by the progress they had made; in fact, they had gone on to his club together afterwards to have a celebratory drink.

No ruder, Annabel supposes, when asked to a theatre of your choice, on the day of your choice, than

smoking a dirty great cigar in a taxi. By the time they reach the restaurant, they can barely see one another through the asphyxiating haze.

George would rather not have a drink at the bar, would prefer to go straight to the table.

'Attractive little place,' he informs the manager. Oddly enough – since it is one of Christina's 'very favourites' – he does not seem to have heard of the restaurant. 'How long have you been open?'

'Four months,' the manager tells him.

'Four months, eh? And still pretty full. A good sign. What about that table over there in the corner?'

'I'm afraid it's reserved, Sir. For another customer. This is your table here, Sir.'

Max looks at the table indicated: it is a perfectly adequate one, it seems to him, with a banquette against the wall and two chairs with their backs to the room.

'Like having dinner in the middle of a public

thoroughfare,' George announces and, producing his wallet, pulls out a five pound note. 'Now, my dear fellow … '

'I'm sorry, Sir, but … '

'But what?'

'It's been specially reserved by another customer.'

For a moment it looks as if George is going to lose his temper. But he doesn't.

'Very well then,' he says, turning to Max. 'If you don't mind, I'd like an upright chair, even if it does mean being knocked off it every two minutes. And Christina, I know, will want to sit on the inside. She likes to see what's going on.'

'Fine,' says Max.

'No harm in trying, eh, old boy?' says George, as they take their seats.

'No.' Max feels uncomfortable. 'I mean, no, I suppose not.'

George would like a dry martini, 'very dry, Gordons of course, on the rocks.' Having stubbed out his half-finished cigar, he puts on his spectacles and turns his attention to the menu.

A young waiter, whom they haven't seen before, brings the drinks.

'And what about this?' George hands him the ashtray with his cigar butt in it.

'Excuse me, Sir,' says the waiter, taking it from him.

George sniffs his drink, scowls at it, calls the young waiter back.

'This isn't Gordons. I asked for Gordons.'

'Gordons?'

'Gordons gin.'

'Excuse me … '

'Do you speak English?'

'Yes, Sir. I take lessons,' the boy stammers, blushing.

'So do you know what gin is?'

'Yes, Sir.'

'And Gordons?'

'Is gin?'

'Precisely. But this isn't Gordons.' George taps his glass. 'I asked for Gordons.'

'I ask … '

'Yes,' Max intervenes. 'Take it back and ask them for Gordons gin. It wasn't you who took the order, I know.'

With a quick look of gratitude, the boy almost snatches George's glass from the table and scuttles off with it.

'You might think,' says George, eyeing a quite pretty woman at the next table, 'that, with unemployment running at its present high level, we might get the odd English-speaking waiter. But no. Oh no, no, no. The British are far too grand nowadays to stoop to anything so low as waiting on their fellow men.'

To Max and Annabel's confusion, the ensuing monologue on the moral decline of the British working class and its acquisition of false values seems to be directed, not so much at them, as at the next table, at the quite pretty woman and, perhaps too, her companion. It is a subject on which George has much to say and the dissertation only stops with the arrival of the head waiter to take their orders for food.

'Have you decided?' Max asks George. 'And what about Mrs Pinkney? Perhaps you'd like to order for her?'

'Christina? She could well be a couple of hours. Now, waiter, this *foie gras de canard* – is it really fresh?'

'Yes, Sir. We have it sent from the Dordogne.'

'Excellent. I shall have it. Don't worry, dear boy, I shall of course pay the extra.'

'Oh no,' Max protests. 'This is on us.'

George beams at the woman at the next table.

'Very kind of you, dear boy,' he says. 'And then, I think the veal with the cream sauce sounds good. Where is your veal from?'

'The veal is Dutch, Sir.'

'Dutch veal, eh? Very good. And what about you, m'dear?' George asks, turning to Annabel.

Since he has obviously taken over the whole business of ordering, Annabel realises that she will

47

have to forego the consultation which she usually has with Max and which is a part of eating in restaurants that they enjoy almost as much as the food itself. Annoyed, however, at being so deprived, she feels suddenly rebellious and says: 'I think, Max, I'd like *moules à la crème* and then veal, the ... '

'Hm. *Moules à la crème* and the veal, eh?' says George loudly. 'Do you think, m'dear, that two cream sauces will ... '

'I was going,' says Annabel, feeling the blood rising hotly to the surface of her skin, 'to have the roast stuffed veal, but ... '

'Of course,' Max interrupts her, before she can say any more. 'My wife would like *moules à la crème* and the roast stuffed veal. And I'll have *quenelles* and the tongue.'

'Very good, Sir. I'll send the wine waiter.'

Annabel is silent. George strums irritably on the table.

'Perhaps,' Max suggests, when the *sommelier* brings him the wine list, 'you had better show it to Mr Pinkney. Would you choose for us? After all, you are a connoisseur.'

'Well, if you'd like me to,' says George; then perks up. 'Of course, I'd be delighted, dear boy.'

The ordering of the wines accomplished, George is reminded of a trip he made through France as an undergraduate, with a couple of Oxford friends. So far as food and wine are concerned, he appears to be blessed – although that is not exactly how either Max or Annabel would have put it – with total recall. They have been on the road for nearly two weeks of lunches and dinners when a flurry near the door announces the arrival of Christina.

'Here's Mrs Pinkney,' says Annabel brightly but, as it turns out, prematurely. Having had a few words with the manager, who hastens outside, Christina sees a group of friends and goes over to their table to talk to them.

'So she is,' says George. 'Well, that evening, at about sevenish, I seem to remember, we got to Cahors, where the truffles ... '

Ten minutes later, as they are approaching Carcassonne, their first course and Christina arrive at the table together.

'Well, hello everybody,' says Christina, looking round the restaurant – to check, presumably, that she hasn't missed any other friends. 'Didn't you see darling Larry, George? He sends his love.'

'Mrs Pinkney!' says the older of the two waiters who are serving them.

'Dieter!'

'Nice to see you.'

'Haven't seen me here before in the evening, have you? What's that George? *Foie gras*?'

'I'm afraid we haven't ordered for you,' Max explains. 'We weren't sure how long you would be.'

'Of course you didn't. Just give me some wine, and I'll have a bit of George's *foie gras*.'

'No you won't. They *say* it's fresh. And you don't really like it anyway.'

'Old meanyboots,' says Christina, sitting down beside Max. 'Dieter – my husband.'

Dieter looks embarrassed, nods politely at George.

Max gives Christina some white wine.

'Well, Dieter,' says Christina. 'If I can't have any of my husband's *foie gras*, what do you suggest.'

'A nice trout perhaps? Or would you prefer to see the menu?'

Christina narrows her eyes, as if trying to conjure up the image of a nice trout.

'Oh no, you know me,' she says at last, coming out of her trance. 'Just give me a grilled sole. On the bone. And *pommes frites*, of course. Done my way.'

'Yes Madam.'

'Well!' Christina sits back, sighs heavily, flicks at her corkscrew curls with her fingertips. They wouldn't, she just knows they couldn't, believe what she has been through. Toots, to begin with, was quite shirty with her. But then actors are so vain and live so close to their work that they often lose all sense of proportion about it. It has taken her some time to make him see that she was only saying what she was saying for the sake of his 'artistic integrity'.

Max and Annabel manage to exchange a quick look without being detected.

'So important,' says Christina, with reverence repeating the word: 'Integrity. Now, come on, George, what about just a tiny bit of that *pâté*?'

Before George can do anything to stop her, she reaches across the table with her knife and, deftly nicking off a small corner of *foie gras,* pops it into her mouth. 'Hm,' she says. 'Delicious. And those *quenelles* look good too. Mind if I try a bit?'

'Of course not,' says Max. 'I'll just give you … '

'Oh, don't bother with that.' This time Christina reaches out with her fork. And is less skilful. The piece of *quenelle* she has skewered breaks in two and falls on to the table. 'Oops,' she says. 'Clumsy': and scrapes the two bits up, leaving a long orangey-pink smear on the tablecloth.

'That's what happens,' says George, evidently amused, 'to people who pick at other people's plates.'

'Oh stop being so stuffy, George.'

George looks positively pleased, as if he might well start to purr.

'Isn't he a darling?' says Christina.

To Max and Annabel's relief, she does not seem to expect a reply.

'A darling,' says Christina again, as the younger of their two waiters clears away their empty plates.

'Would you care to taste the red wine?' the *sommelier* asks Max. 'Or will Mr Pinkney?'

'Mr Pinkney, please.'

The couple at the next table are getting ready to leave. George tries to catch the woman's eye, says to the wine waiter in his special carrying voice: 'Haven't finished my white yet. Be a good chap and do it for us, eh?'

'Me, Sir?'

'Don't tell me you don't know what that thing you're wearing round your neck is for?'

'I know, Sir, but … '

'Come on then. Have a tipple on us.'

'Very well, Sir.'

With obvious reluctance, the *sommelier* does as he has been told.

'And how is it?'

'I think you will like it, Sir.'

'Excellent.' George swivels round in his chair. To see if the couple at the next table have seen all this, Annabel supposes? But they are already at the far end of the restaurant.

'What is it, George?' Christina asks.

'Nothing, m'dear. Nothing.'

And so the evening continues. Upon the arrival of his main course George feels compelled to give Dieter a lecture on the raising of veal. In his opinion, it is the Japanese who these days do it best, Christina's *pommes frites* are sent back to the kitchen, to be 'put in very hot oil again, for just a minute or two,' because they are not quite how she likes them, not quite up to the usual standard. Now that George has lost his audience at the next table, he remembers that there is to be a sales conference while he is away and plunges into a long business conversation with Max. After eating about a quarter of her sole, Christina orders a pack of cigarettes ('That reminds me, George, I had to get the restaurant to pay my taxi'). Having lit a cigarette, she screws up the outer cellophane wrapping from the packet and puts it in the ashtray, where it slowly uncoils again; and when, a few minutes later, George lights his next cigar, the match, not properly extinguished, sets fire to the cellophane, Christina pours her wine all over it and the table, and a waiter has to be called to clean up the mess.

No, nobody would like even a sorbet. Just coffee – decaffeinated for Christina, regular for George. Liqueurs would be 'most acceptable, dear boy,' and 'heaven'.

Annabel, meanwhile, has been hearing, and is still hearing, about Christina's 'work': which is for her both 'an act of expiation' and 'a celebration', the only way in which 'I feel I can rise above my day-to-day existence' and, at the same time, 'if you like, atone'.

But then Annabel too must have felt that extraordinary urge to cleanse herself – it's so wonderful, isn't it, when it really comes off, like having a baby (Christina imagines, since she hasn't had any), or perhaps (a look of rapture illuminates her face) 'a really good shit'? Annabel hasn't experienced that feeling? Well, never mind, it will come to her, it will be the most important thing in her life, Christina can tell. Her work – her poetry, at any rate – is, she has to admit, rather avant-garde: not at all George's cup of tea, but then he doesn't read much these days anyhow. So unlike her darling second husband. He had been such a help to her. He it was who had compared her to a medieval alchemist searching for the philosopher's stone, which in her case meant 'the perfect form': the form which would enable her 'to summon up simultaneously not just a part, but the whole world of the mind and the senses', and so 'to mirror the way in which we communicate with one another', it seems to her, 'through the unconscious, through the vibrations transmitted and received by our instinctive selves, our true animal selves'.

Had George not been Max's employer, Annabel would almost certainly by now have asked him if he could try to manipulate his cigar in such a way as to prevent her from being enveloped, at regular intervals, in the wreaths of smoke that are making her head spin; and had Christina not been George's wife, she might even have told her that she found her ideas both pretentious and commonplace, and her intensity as nauseating, in its own way, as her husband's cigar smoke. As it was, however, she did neither; she simply sat there, occasionally nodding, as Christina moved on from her poetry to her ambition to adapt books 'that I particularly adore, that touch that special chord in me' for the medium, in which, after all, she had grown up: 'the magical world of the theatre.' Several attempts, Annabel learns, have been made at realising this ambition: darling Toots had particularly admired Christina's stage version of *The Waves*, ('so sensitive,' he had said, 'so quite unlike anything else'); and yet, even with her connections, it has so far proved impossible to 'get anything off the ground'. But now, though, she has a wonderful idea. She is so excited, she can hardly wait to get her teeth into it. Has Annabel by any chance read Diana Petre's *Secret Orchard*?

As a matter of fact, Annabel has; and she has also seen and very much enjoyed a television adaptation of it.

So, 'Yes – and I thought they did it very well on television,' she tells Christina, wondering if, even at this late hour, she might not be able to get her to talk about something other than her own literary output. 'Didn't you?'

Christina looks annoyed.

'Unfortunately, I missed it,' she says airily. 'I'm told it wasn't bad and I shall, of course, have to see it. But my approach will be quite different. Although I haven't met her yet, I intend … '

Is it possible that Christina has noticed the look of disbelief which Annabel is unable to suppress on hearing that her 'approach' is going to be 'quite different' from what she has not even seen? Or is it something else?

'George darling,' Christina exclaims suddenly, interrupting herself in mid-sentence, no longer interested, apparently, in disclosing to Annabel her plans for Mrs Petre and her book. 'Do you know what time it is? We were supposed to be at Effie's an hour ago.'

'Well, in that case,' says George, with evident satisfaction, 'we're too late.'

'But George, we *have* to go, darling. After all, we *are* staying with them in Spetsai. And you know Effie *adores* you.'

'Does she?' It is not so much that George seems to doubt this adoration, rather that he is indifferent to it. 'So far as I'm concerned, I'm ready for bed.'

'Well, if you won't, I still have to,' says Christina. 'Impossible, isn't he? So naughty,' she adds, appealing first to Max, then to Annabel.

'I'll get the bill,' says Max, scarcely able to believe

their luck. 'Unless you'd like another calvados, of course?' he asks George.

Their luck holds.

'No, thank you, no, dear boy. They take it out of an old man like me, you know, these big committee meetings.'

'Poor old George,' says Christina. 'He so loves them. Just look at him!'

Both Max and Annabel try to avoid doing so.

'Would you mind terribly, you two,' Christina asks, 'if I rush? I'm so late for darling Effie and the bills here can take for ever.'

Annabel, fearing that she might overdo it, lets Max answer for both of them.

'Of course not.'

'You're an angel. Both of you: angels.' With a quick flick at her curls, Christina seizes her bag and is on her feet. Kiss kiss; kiss kiss; kiss kiss – the last of these for George. 'Oh and, darling, you'd better give me some money.'

George takes out his wallet, gives her a couple of five pound notes.

'Lovely, darling. And a heavenly dinner, thank you so much,' says Christina, blowing extravagant kisses at Max and at Annabel. 'Goodbye,' she calls out to Dieter and his acolyte, who are attending to a table some three or four away from them. 'Goodbye, Dieter. Goodbye, Bertrand. See you in September.'

Several people turn round in their seats, to see what is going on.

'Goodbye, Mrs Pinkney. Have a good holiday.'

'Well, *ciao*, everybody, I must rush,' says Christina and, with a toss of her Medusa-like locks, heads for the door.

With Christina gone, George seems to sink into an abstracted reverie, from which neither Max nor Annabel makes any attempt to recall him. Not until the bill has been settled and the tip taken away does he show any sign of animation.

'Time to go, eh?' he says then, stifling a yawn.

In the street he still appears to be half-asleep.

55

Max flags down a cab, gives the driver the Pinkneys' address.

'Thank you, dear boy, thank you,' says George climbing in through the door, which Max is holding open for him. 'And you too, m'dear,' he adds, making what is clearly an effort to pull himself together. 'A most acceptable dinner – although I have to tell you I wasn't altogether sure about the *foie gras*. But never mind, eh, old boy? I know a little place. When I get back we'll have a spot of lunch.'

'That would be very nice.'

'Poor, poor Max,' says Annabel, as the cab pulls away from them. 'But at least with *him*, I suppose, you can talk business? And what about the old cow's taxi fare and her fags? I bet they were down on the bill.'

'Of course. Not that it made much difference.'

'Do we have to do it often?' Annabel wonders.

'Never again,' says Max. 'I promise. I'd rather get another job. Even emigrate.'

Five

HOSPITAL VISITS

'Visit briefly, cheerfully, and leave the patient rested and encouraged.' – *The New Emily Post's Etiquette,* Elizabeth L. Post, 1975.

Bunny

Ever since you first noticed the lump, what you dreaded almost as much as the possibility of its being malignant was the thought that, if you did have to have an operation, you might afterwards be visited in hospital by Bunny. Bunny whom you have known since childhood. Dear Bunny (a plain, dumpy girl, with a bad complexion, she had especially enjoyed dressing up, making up and doing wildly exaggerated 'impersonations'), kind Bunny (she never forgot a birthday), poor Bunny (no man had ever seemed to notice that Bunny was a woman, at least not in the way that Bunny, in earlier days anyway, had sometimes admitted that she might have liked).

Dear, kind, poor old Bunny – but by your bedside, when you had no means of escaping her, definitely no. So you proceeded stealthily. About the lump and about your suspicions about the lump, you told her nothing; and then, when you learned that the tumour was almost certainly benign but must still be removed, when they let you know when the hospital could take you in, you told her that you were going away for a week or so. You even said you would miss her; which, in a sense, was true. More than once, in the three days since the operation, you have congratulated yourself on the success of this more or less white lie. What you will tell her on your return from your stay away doesn't seem to matter. And now, suddenly, at half-past two in the afternoon, a good half-hour before visiting time, when most of the patients in your

57

ward are dozing and you yourself are comfortably drowsing – now you hear her, in the distance maybe, but unmistakeably.

'A few minutes perhaps. But if you say she hasn't got it, what difference does that make?'

You pull the bedclothes over your head. As if that could help.

Clack, clack, clack – can she be wearing golf shoes?

'Or aren't you sure?' Bunny's voice rings out loud and clear, in no way muffled by the sheets about your ears. 'Did they do proper tests?'

But Bunny doesn't play golf, or indeed go in for any kind of sport.

'Aha.' For a moment, the clacking stops. 'Where is she then? That one? Right.'

Clack, clack, clack and CLACK. Something heavy lands on your feet. The metal bed rattles. Pretending to have been asleep, with a yawn, you turn over, lowering the bedclothes.

Bunny is examining the progress chart attached to the foot of your bed.

'Bunny,' you say weakly, trying to feign pleasure. After all, she is your oldest friend. She means well.

Bunny looks up from the chart, scrutinises your face. Slowly, her own screws itself up, so that her nose becomes huge, her eyes tiny.

'But, darling,' she says at last, 'you look dreadful. Like death.'

With a clatter, she drops the chart and advances round the side of the bed. Clack, clack. Then she hesitates. She is wearing some kind of ethnic blanket, with a hole in it for her head. Her shoes, though, look quite ordinary.

'You should have told me,' she explodes, seizing your hand and squeezing it tightly in her own. 'Oh, darling.' Her eyes mist over. Please God don't let Bunny start wailing.

'I didn't want you to worry,' you venture.

Bunny's mouth drops open, closes for a moment, then opens again.

'You don't want me to worry!'

Before you know what is happening, Bunny is beside you on the bed and your head, snatched up off the pillow, is buried in the very scratchy ethnic blanket, being wrenched – Bunny would no doubt have said 'rocked' – from side to side.

Bunny's grip is a powerful one. Speech is impossible, suffocation imminent. You could try biting her.

Suddenly, with no more warning than when she flung her arms, mother-bear-like, around you, she lets you go. You drop back, panting, on to your pillows.

'I've brought you these,' booms Bunny, picking up off your feet and flourishing an enormous bunch of florist-wrapped, and therefore invisible, flowers.

'How kind,' you murmur, unable to admire what you cannot see. 'You shouldn't have … '

59

Bunny is no longer with you. At the far end of the ward, she has spotted a nurse.

'I say,' she cries. 'I say, Nurse, what about something to put these in?'

From thirty beds – no, twenty-nine, Mrs Swartout died in the night and her bed is still empty – those patients who are not already riveted by the performance of your visitor raise themselves on to their elbows, some reaching for their spectacles, to see what is going on.

'For these,' bawls Bunny, ripping away green waxy paper to reveal a strident display of magenta, puce and knicker-pink gladioli. 'A vase with some water.'

'I'm afraid,' says the nurse, hastening up, on silent feet, a finger to her lips, 'we haven't got anything big enough at the moment. But if you'll … '

'Nothing big enough!' Bunny ignores the nurse's admonition, makes no concession to the dimunition of the distance between herself and her interlocutor. 'But that's ridiculous.'

'It's why we advise pot plants,' the nurse explains, with a side-long glance at you, clearly asking for help. 'They're less trouble. Somehow vases tend to get smashed – or in the way.'

'Do they indeed,' says Bunny. 'And what about that one?'

Since you know (as the nurse has sensed) that there is no way of deflecting Bunny from her purpose, you can only watch, mesmerised, as she strides down the ward to accost a frail, mousey-haired little woman, on whose bedside table there stands a jug of lilies, slightly yellowing admittedly, but still by no means dead.

'You don't mind, do you?' Bunny asks the woman, holding up the jug for those about her to see. 'After all, these are finished. And you have that pretty azalea.' (In fact, it's a cineraria.) 'Very pretty.'

The woman does not protest.

'Here,' says Bunny, handing the jug to the nurse. 'If you'd just throw these out and put in some fresh water.'

60

Obediently, the nurse pads off on her errand.

All eyes are on Bunny.

'Well,' she says, rubbing the palms of her hands over her skirt before plonking herself down again on your bed. 'What I need now is a cigarette.'

From the floor she produces a lumpy canvas holdall you hadn't noticed before. In it is her bag and in her bag are her cigarettes.

'But, Buns,' you remind her, 'This is a cancer ward. Smoking ... '

'What, all of them?' Bunny exclaims, looking round the ward at first one of your fellow patients, then another. Mrs Mullaney, who has been in the bed next to yours since she had a masectomy the day before yesterday, is subjected to a particularly long stare.

'How ghastly,' says Bunny at last. 'But thank God, darling, *you* haven't got it.'

With a deep and protracted sigh, Bunny returns her cigarettes to her bag and her bag to the holdall. This reminds her that she has cooked you some special dishes ('because of the filth they always give you in these places'); but, before she can unpack it, the nurse is back. It is well after three o'clock now and quite a number of other visitors are huddled round the beds of their friends or relatives.

'Well done,' Bunny tells the nurse and, scooping together the several unwieldy bunches of 'glads', eventually succeeds in cramming the whole lot of them, string and all, into the jug. Even she seems somewhat startled by the result.

'Never was much good at that kind of thing, was I?' she says. Having made room for her monster porcupine arrangement by removing your books, glasses, fruit and bottles of lemon squash on to the floor, she loses interest in it. 'Cooking though, that's another matter,' she announces cheerfully, returning to the holdall.

Various mousses, a cold fish salad, a terrine – or so Bunny says, the food is in silver-foil containers, on which she explains she had meant to stick labels – all of these are laid out on your bed. But the *pièce de résistance* is a 'simply marvellous chocolate concoction, it'll go round everybody'. And that, with Bunny making the most of this opportunity to have what she would doubtless have called 'a few words' with each of your fellow patients and their visitors, is just what it does.

A welcome break, you think at first, as she clumps purposefully off, cake and a red-handled camp-knife in hand. But you hadn't reckoned with the snippets of Bunny's jovial banter which, try as you may, you cannot help overhearing. 'Will-power, that's what'll cure you sooner than anything. Mind over matter.' Or 'Catholic are you? … Methodist? … Oh well, I've never been anti-Semitic.' Or 'No, that's my friend over there. She hasn't got it, I'm pleased to say. Just a small operation.' And so on. And so on. Last, about an hour and a half later, comes Mrs Mullaney, in the bed next to yours. By now most of the visitors have left. In a few minutes the doctors will be doing their rounds. Mrs Mullaney doesn't want any cake.

'Come on. It's delicious. It'll do you good.' Bunny is about to slide the unwelcome treat on to Mrs Mullaney's bedside table.

'No, really, thank you. I've never eaten sweet things.'

'Not even when you were a child?'

'It would be a waste.'

'Well yes, I suppose it would be,' says Bunny, prepared apparently to be convinced by this argument but by no means at a loss. 'I know what. I've got some excellent jellied consommé I made.'

'Honestly, I'm not hungry. It's very kind of you though.'

'For later then,' says Bunny, depositing what remains of the cake on its board on the bed beside you and sorting through the foil boxes. 'Rotten luck' – evidently, she thinks she is whispering; she winks at you and rolls her eyes to indicate Mrs Mullaney behind her. 'Even so, masectomies always remind me of something I read somewhere about asymmetrical bodies. This wretched woman was worried about having to have the operation and her husband – or was it her lover? I don't remember – anyway, he insisted that, if she had to have one off, she must have the other off as well.'

Having divined, in the nick of time, the direction in which Bunny's story was going, you have tried to drown her last words with a bout of coughing. Whether or not Mrs Mullaney has heard her, you cannot tell; but Bunny, you see, has screwed up her face again, has put on her concerned look.

'It was in the breast, wasn't it?' she asks meaningly.

'It was.'

'And you're all right. Of course you are. Aha, here it is.'

She has found the consommé and is about to go in search of a spoon – with which, presumably, to force-feed Mrs Mullaney – when she remembers something.

'But I haven't told you, have I,' she says, 'how I found out you were in here?'

'No. No, you haven't.'

Does it matter? Here she is. And that's that.

'Well, since you're all right, I suppose I'd better tell you,' Bunny says ominously. 'Or perhaps I shouldn't?'

'Now that you've started … '

'You're sure it won't upset you?'

This is too much.

'If you won't tell me what it is, how can I say?'

Bunny is offended.

'There's no need to snap at me,' she snaps; then is ashamed of herself. 'I'm sorry,' she says. 'It was Charley.'

Charley is – or was? yes, clearly was – your cat: an old cat, certainly, too old you know some people thought, but that doesn't make any difference. Like a child, you begin to sob, as Bunny cradles your head in her arms once more, telling you how your cleaning woman, when she went to feed him, found him dead; how she had telephoned Bunny; how she had felt she ought to tell Bunny where you really were. Dimly, you hear a nurse telling Bunny that visiting hours are over; less dimly, you hear Bunny telling the nurse that she has no intention of leaving you in your present condition.

Then your doctor is there.

'What's all this about?' he asks Bunny as much as you, his eyebrows shooting up from behind his spectacle frames.

'She's upset,' Bunny explains in a schoolmistressy way. 'Because I had to tell her that her cat had died.'

'He was old anyway,' you say, grateful for the doctor's presence, still more grateful that this presence

seems to have suggested to Bunny that she should think about going. She has released you from her embrace and is doing up the zipper on her holdall.

'Perhaps it might have been better to let her find out later,' the doctor says, quite mildly, but there is no mistaking the note of criticism in his voice.

For a moment Bunny seems to accept the rebuke. But only for a moment.

'No, I don't think so,' she tells the doctor, squaring up to him, slinging the holdall over her shoulder. 'Since you say she's okay, it was best to do as I did. Now what I want to ask you is about the tests. My friend's brother-in-law is a cancer specialist and she tells me … '

'I'm sorry,' the doctor interrupts her. 'We don't discuss our patients either in front … '

'Oh, come on,' says Bunny. 'I'm her oldest … '

'Even so … '

'Well, in that case – just a minute.' Bunny reaches down and gives you a businesslike peck on each cheek. 'Goodbye, darling, don't worry about anything,' she tells you. 'I'll be back tomorrow. I promise.'

To your astonishment, the doctor allows himself to be taken by the elbow and propelled down the ward in the direction of the door.

'The trouble is,' Bunny can be heard telling him, 'according to my friend's brother-in-law, with the old tests you can never be quite certain. He even knows of cases where people have been told they are okay and then have died – of cancer, of course – in a matter of months. Now with these new tests – Cobbold, are they called? I can find out. Or are those what you gave her?' At last, at long last, finally, her voice is trailing away into the distance. 'You see what I really must know is … '

All you can hear now is the clacking of her shoes.

'Wow,' says Mrs Mullaney.

'Yes. I'm sorry. Of course she means well,' you hear yourself saying, for the umpteenth time, about dear, kind, poor old Bunny. But is that, the disloyal thought suddenly strikes you, enough?

'Far too often visitors to hospitals are thoughtless and careless,' says Emily Post: so here, for potential Bunnies of either sex, are a few helpful hints gleaned from 'the most reliable and up-to-date authority for the social customs of the 1970s (i.e. *The New Emily Post's Etiquette*).

'Courtesy to nurses and the other hospital personnel, quietness of manner and approach in the hospital buildings, avoidance of asking for special attention from busy people, are obvious requirements.

'Don't bring as your gift foods that the patient may not be permitted to have, unless you have first checked with his physician or nurse.

'Don't talk about his illness in front of the patient.

Ask for the necessary information, from those who are competent to give it, out of the patient's hearing and sight.

'Don't worry a patient about anything that you feel might upset or disturb him. The best thing you can do, if you wish his speedy return home, is to bring him cheerful, encouraging news that will make him want to get there quickly.

'Don't overstay your welcome.

'If another patient in a room wishes to rest, draw the curtains between the beds to give him as much privacy and quiet as possible. On the other hand, if he and your friend have become friendly, include him in the conversation and your visit will be doubly appreciated.

'Voices must naturally be kept lower, not only for privacy's sake, but in order not to disturb the other sick people who may badly need their rest.

'Whenever it is possible, bring flowers in their own container and let them be of a size that can be easily handled.'

And last, 'Don't think that the hospital routine has been devised to bedevil you as a visitor, or the patient himself.... Limited visiting hours, early meals, and rules governing smoking may seem unreasonable to you, but you must remember that they have not been made just for the benefit of your sister Susie, who may have nothing more than a broken leg, but rather for the sicker patients, who without a carefully planned routine and the best possible conditions for rest and quiet might not recover at all.'

Some people positively enjoy the atmosphere of a hospital; others do not care for it at all. Charlotte Ford is one of the latter, tending 'to become a patient myself when I'm confronted with someone connected to tubes or just someone who is obviously sick'. Since her visit wouldn't 'help either of us', she prefers to 'call and ask how I can help'. Should you be like Ms. Ford, she suggests that 'you might offer to feed the cat, postpone appointments or bring drugstore items to the hospital.'

Six

RELATIONS

'The welcome houseguest is, above all else, adaptable.' - *The New Emily Post's Etiquette*, Elizabeth L. Post, 1975.
'We make our friends; God makes our relations.'
– Simon Raven

Deirdre and David

Every January, after Christmas and New Year with her cousins in Scotland, Deirdre and David leave England to winter in warmer parts. This year they have been to New Zealand to stay for eight out of ten weeks with David's newly-remarried elder sister, Elspeth. On their way back from Auckland, they break their journey in Los Angeles to spend a week with David's much younger half-sister, Liz, and her husband, Harry Scott. Three years ago it had been the Scotts' turn to provide winter sunshine for Deirdre and David (they had, amongst other things, done Disneyland, been up the coast and down the coast and into the desert). Remembering how near to going crazy both he and Liz had become by the end of that visit, Harry decides that this time he will keep a day-to-day record of what precisely it is that Liz's brother and his wife do that can turn a reasonably ordinary, easy-going sort of a household – or so it seems to the Scotts to be – upside down.

The Journal

March 31
Day 1. Morning off work to meet them. (Trouble last time because Liz went without me. David, 'with his heart', had to get the cases into the trunk.) It isn't their fault that their flight gets in at 7 a.m. and we

have to be up at six. Kids still asleep. They can get their own breakfast. Lois will pick them up for school. We are pulling out of the driveway when Liz remembers there are a lot of her clothes in the guest-room closet. (Trouble about this, too, last time.) She runs back and fetches them into our room. She has flung them all on the bed, she says.

We are on time. The flight is not. (Should have called the airport first.) At 9.30 the plane lands and, forty minutes later, out comes a trolley-load of strapped leather baggage, with David scarcely visible

behind it and Madam Gracious floating along beside it, a couple of fur coats hanging over her arm. As usual the hair is immaculately swept into place and the make-up expertly applied. But underneath the paint there are signs of strain. 'That's more than just jet-lag,' I said to Liz.

'Getting older.'

Effusive greetings. As usual they insisted on calling Liz Elizabeth and me Harrison. (Liz must have told them a hundred times how I hate to be called Harrison.) We both looked 'so well'. The flight had been 'beastly', we 'simply couldn't imagine how frightful'. I took charge of the trolley, brought the car round, packed in their stuff. Deirdre didn't care to have her furs put in the trunk. She preferred to keep them with her.

Elspeth, it seemed, had 'done them pretty well'. Her new husband, Hubert, (they'd met him before, 'in London, of course'), was a 'splendid fellow', said David. Deirdre had found him 'perfectly charming', with 'those marvellous manners that are so rare even in England these days'. (And in the United States, she seemed to be saying, quite unknown. Paranoia?) Hubert and Elspeth's apartment was both 'enormous' (being three apartments knocked into one) and 'enchanting', with 'panoramic views of the harbour'. Hubert and Elspeth had servants. In the city they had Filipinos. The food had been 'excellent', not only in Auckland, but on the farm, where it was prepared by an Indonesian couple. It was 'something of a bore for Elspeth', Deirdre supposed, that the Indonesian couple and the two Filipinos didn't get on. But then servants were like that and it didn't work out too badly really, having one lot in the city and another on the farm. It was only occasionally, after all, that it might have been convenient to have had them all in one place. For big parties and that sort of thing. There had been a lot of big parties. Considering how far away from everything they lived, New Zealanders were 'really rather civilized'. It was a good life out there, in David's opinion: not too many people,

70

beautiful countryside and a perfect climate. He had got in a week's trout-fishing at Taupo and Hubert had taken him out 'after the big boys' in the Bay of Islands.

'Well, life's rather different here, as you know,' Liz said, as we pulled up outside the house. 'Not even one Filipino. I hope you won't find it too difficult to adjust?'

Deirdre smiled frostily out of the window, survey-ing the garden with her connoisseur's eye. Last visit she was full of suggestions. None of these has been implemented. The camellia bush whose planting she supervised (standing by, giving me instructions) went yellow and died a couple of years back.

David was 'quite prepared', he said, 'to take the rough with the smooth'. After all, Elspeth's hospitali-ty had been 'for this day and age quite exceptional'. It would do them good to get back to reality.

Deirdre coughed a dry little cough. There were very definite limits, the cough said, to the amount of 'reality' that Madam G. could be expected to put up with.

However, aside from a shortage of hangers in the guest-room, both lunch and the rest of the day seem to have gone off okay. Probably because they were tired. When I came back from an afternoon checking some properties, they were still resting. And they went to bed early.

Talk still mostly about New Zealand – backed up with a stack of photographs. (In one or two of these Elspeth and her new husband couldn't help looking pretty much how we reckoned they must have felt at having David and Madam G. as their guests for eight weeks.) At dinner Deirdre even complimented Liz on the fish – although she did go on to say she thought 'a touch of dill wouldn't have done any harm'. Only really bad moment was when Deirdre produced presents for the kids. When Jeff found he'd been given a fluffy bear, it didn't need any mind-reader to tell what he thought of people who brought that sort of thing to a nine-year-old boy. Luckily, though, Kelly

liked hers so much it almost made up for it. She says she's going to buy it some clothes.

Why does Deirdre have a special voice for talking to kids? It's not as if she'd never had a child of her own. Or was she like that with Caroline? (Oh yes, we were shown pictures too of Caroline's baby and told a lot about what a good baby it was, what a good marriage Caroline had made, how 'brilliantly' the husband was doing etc. etc.)

'And now we're six, aren't we?' Deirdre said to Kelly, in this coy little voice, when she first came in to say hello to her. 'And how do we like being six?' Since she was only five about a month back, probably Kelly was flattered. At any rate, she didn't say anything. She gave Deirdre a weird look and from then onwards, till she got the bear, did her best to avoid her.

April 3.

No time to do this since Tuesday.

Day 2. Still a bit jet-lagged, which may have helped in a way. At least we didn't have to play bridge. Liz knows their morning routine backwards by now. In London it seems that, since David retired, he gets up at about nine, has a bath, is given breakfast by the daily help, does his correspondence and then goes out to his club. Madam has breakfast in bed at half-past ten, seldom emerges from her room until midday. Here they do much the same, except that Liz is the 'daily help'. Breakfast for me and the kids at 8, for David at 9.30, for Deirdre at 10.30.

Complaints (David a.m.): Why in a state full of fresh oranges can't 'one' have freshly-squeezed orange juice? Why do American eggs have so little flavour? Is that why their yolks are so pale? Why are the newspapers so parochial? Or don't people here take any interest in international affairs? (All familiar. Same as last time. Liz has made a note to get oranges.)

Suggestions (Deirdre p.m.): Couldn't Liz find someone – 'perhaps a coloured woman or one of those Mexican immigrants we're always hearing about' – to help her in the house? She seems to have 'so much to do always' and 'surely you must be able to afford it these days?' Wouldn't it be 'a good idea' to keep out the neighbours' dogs (Deirdre had spotted one of these taking a shit on the grass outside her bedroom window) by putting a gate at the bottom of the driveway? And what about Jeffrey's hair? Wasn't it 'just a tiny bit too long for a boy'? For lunch, apparently, they started with home-made gazpacho. Deirdre told Liz she must remind her to send 'a simply marvellous new recipe I've got for gazpacho. You wouldn't believe it could taste so good.'

After lunch came gardening hints. To kill the next couple of hours Liz took them for a ride by the ocean, pointing out to them, she says, things she knew they'd seen before, so as to avoid having to listen to them. Then came 'forty winks' for David in the sitting room, and for Deirdre 'my rest' in the guest-room. From these they were both awoken by Jeff and the kids from next door playing tether-ball. Not popular, Liz says, but nobody was actually bawled out. By the time I got back they were all dressed up as if they were going to a party, and ready for their gin. In New Zealand, at Elspeth's and Hubert's, it seems everyone 'dresses for dinner'. But they know we don't. And why didn't they do it the night before? Anyway, the sight of Deirdre looking like that sent Liz scooting off to change her dress and I backed her up by getting into a jacket and tie. They'd also 'forgotten' – or so Deirdre pretended – that we always have our evening meal at 7.30 because of the kids. Hubert's daughter-in-law feeds her children first, then packs them off to bed with a book, as Deirdre used to do with Caroline. But of course people in California don't read books, do they? They're so addicted to television. 'What's the matter with TV?' Jeff wanted to know, but before Deirdre could get her teeth into him Liz managed to get him out of the room.

Towards the end of dinner (always wine with them here, they 'expect' it), especially when the kids had gone next door, things got a bit easier. But, with a few scotches inside him, David's rosy schoolboy face began to go still redder than usual and he suddenly started sounding off about the 'American mania for analysis'. What got him on to that I don't know: because Liz only saw the analyst three times, and that was a couple of years back, after the miscarriage, when she didn't feel like eating. At any rate, he got so worked up about it and ranted so much about 'lack of character' and 'crooked little madmen' who set up as psychiatrists that in the end even Deirdre (had she put him up to it?) saw that it was time to get him to bed.

'All right he was drunk *then*,' Liz said afterwards. 'But he wasn't drunk yesterday, or this afternoon, was he? So it can't be paranoia, can it? And it can't be just because we're so much younger than they are. I really do believe they hate it here. Both of them. So why do they come?'

Day 3. At breakfast, Liz reckons, David must have had remorse. Because although he didn't go so far as to apologise (Liz has never known him do that, except to Deirdre) he kept up a constant barrage of puns and those strange schoolboy-type jokes he likes to make. The weather was so perfect he'd like to take Liz and Deirdre out to lunch, he said. But Liz still had more cooking to do for the party we were pretty sure they'd be expecting us to give for them. And then there were the flowers and things. So David read the paper a bit and followed her about a bit, whistling through his teeth and making his little jokes.

Deirdre, when she showed up, was on form. She didn't mind our party, she told Liz. (If she knew how little anyone else was looking forward to it: after the last visit, Liz had thought it best to warn the other guests what they might be in for.) But 'poor David' was so exhausted after all the parties they had had to go to in New Zealand and she had so much to do when she got back to England, all they really wanted to do was relax. She did hope we wouldn't be going out too much – to dinners with other people or anything like that? Liz had to admit that we'd all been asked (because we'd begged them to do it for us) to the Blomfelds' on Saturday night and to a brunch at Ted and Lois's (they'd met them last time, seemed to get on fairly okay) on Sunday. Couldn't we at least get out of the brunch, Deirdre wondered? She did so hate brunches. Unfortunately, it was too late, Liz told her. For the rest of us anyway. 'But you remember Lois, don't you? She's the one who's keen on fishing. She and David talked for hours about flies and chalk streams, or whatever fishermen talk about together. And they go to England quite often.'

If Deirdre did remember, she wasn't letting on. Instead, she asked if it mightn't be 'a good idea' if, after lunch, she 'had a go' at the flowers, 'tried to cheer them up a bit?' Liz would have liked to strangle her, she says, but she thought it might be a good way of keeping Madam quiet. And it did. Until the kids got back. Then, Deirdre seems to have started needling Kelly (not for the first time). Or maybe Kelly said something fresh to Deirdre. There are two versions of what happened. At any rate, it ended up by Kelly telling Deirdre she was an old bitch and how we all hated them being here. (Would I like to have seen that.) Deirdre outraged and squawking like a panicked chicken, says Liz. She'd never been spoken to like that before, not by anybody, let alone by David's niece, a child who really might have been expected 'to know better'. It took Liz a good hour to calm her down; which put her behind, of course, with her plans for dinner. Then she had to call Lois, who came right over, helped her pack up the kids' things and took them back with her to her place, to keep them out of the way till after Madam's departure. David embarrassed by all this but couldn't persuade Madam to say goodbye even to Jeff. ('They're your relations, not mine,' Liz heard her telling him. 'And they're both as poisonous as each other. Since nobody has bothered to teach them any manners, I see no reason why I should be forced to have anything to do with either of them.')

David at dinner very relaxed, especially with Lois. Madam G. as immaculate as ever, and as uptight and as stuck-up. She had a migraine, she explained, right away, at the beginning. Before dinner was through, it had become so 'splitting' that she was afraid she'd have to 'slip away'. With her safely out of the way, David decided to make a night of it by really hitting the bottle. No aggression though. 'Quite a guy, David,' Gaby Blomfeld said to me on the porch. 'We'll have to get in plenty of booze for Saturday. But, Liz's sister-in-law,' he asked, lowering his voice, 'does she know anyone in England who isn't royal or something?' 'Oh, a few people, I think,' I told him. He saw I was joking. And it is funny: Liz says Deirdre keeps joining these needlepoint charities and things in the hope of getting to know royalties; to date, so far as Liz can make out, she's once shaken hands with some royal duchess and once been in the same reception-hall as that Princess Margaret of theirs who was over here a while back.

76

Day 4. Liz beginning to hate New Zealand. David wanted to take them out 'somewhere quiet, with a view perhaps' for lunch. So they went to the little restaurant in Malibu. And in the afternoon walked by the ocean. None of it up to New Zealand standards.

This evening, dinner later (by special request: 'since the children have gone to stay with their friends'). Afterwards, tried to get out of bridge by suggesting *Citizen Kane* on TV. But Deirdre had seen it so many times, she didn't think she could 'face it' again. It was so long since they'd had a game, what with all those farewell parties in New Zealand. And David did so miss it.

Out came the card table, and for two and a half hours we sat there listening to David drumming his fingers on the table and doing that toothy whistling of his. As Liz said last time, it's difficult to know which of them drives you crazier. David takes so long to decide what to play that by the time he does put down a card you've as good as forgotten everything that's happened before. Madam on the other hand is quick as a rattlesnake, with this horrible habit of pulling out a card long before it's her turn and holding it there – as if to say she's so smart she knows damned well what everyone else is going to play. It makes you want to throw down any old card, just so long as it's not what she's expecting. And then the postmortems: she can't let a hand go by without she has to tell everybody exactly where they went wrong, exactly what they should have done.

'Thank God I didn't make her cancel tomorrow's dinner,' Liz said just now. 'Or we'd be in for another four nights of it.'

April 5.
Day 5. See what Liz means about the afternoons. And about New Zealand. Morning and lunch okay – if you don't mind, that is, being treated like some poor dumb animal who can't be expected to understand anything much about civilized human behaviour. After lunch Liz pretended to have some marketing to

do ('How is it they can turn us into a pair of lying conspirators in our own house?' – in fact she was going round to Lois's with some things for the kids) and I took them on a tour of Beverly Hills. All very 'brash' and 'artificial'. New Zealand had been 'so unpretentious,' 'so exactly the right scale' Deirdre couldn't even see the funny side of it. She sat in the back, with a permanent sneer fixed on her face, and on the way home David gave me a lecture on the difference between our sort of conversation and the European variety. Gist of what he had to say seemed to be as follows: in Europe conversation has been got down to such a fine art that people very seldom mean what they appear to be saying: it's a kind of game; which makes it difficult for Americans, who are so straightforward (i.e. simpleminded, though he didn't say it) to understand Europeans. And vice-versa. Silly prick.

But at least David makes an effort to get on with people – even if he does have to do most of the laughing at his jokes. Martha Blomfeld put on a pretty good show: great food and plenty of booze. Only trouble was she'd invited an English couple. She'd thought they'd like that. And David did. He and this English guy kept on at each other all evening. But Madam took against the wife, who came from Surbiton, she said on the way home – and that clearly was very bad. 'Who's Surrey now?' David sang and doubled up laughing. (Liz explained later; Surbiton is the kind of suburban place in Surrey, outside London, whose inhabitants people like Deirdre like to look down on. In fact the woman told Liz she came from Cheshire, about two hundred miles from London.) So 'appalling' had it been for Madam to be 'cornered' by the woman from Surbiton that she had actually found it 'quite a relief' to get away and talk to 'that funny little Gaby, What's-his-name – you know, our host'.

Day 6. Lois's brunch. Since Madam insisted on having her usual breakfast at the usual time ('After all, we're going to have to be up at the crack of dawn for our plane on Tuesday, aren't we?'), we all had to hang about while she took her bath, dressed, put on her warpaint, etc. – and set off about an hour later than we'd agreed the night before. David as annoyed as anybody, but it wasn't worth trying to hustle her, he said. Not that it mattered being late, because it was a barbecue by the pool. Quite a few people and lots of kids. Right away David weighed into the Bloody Bulls (hadn't heard of them before) and, after three or four of them, was in the pool organising some kind of water-polo for the kids and shouting to us all to come and join them.

'Well, at least *he* seems to be enjoying himself,' Lois said.

Madam had found a patch of shade under an umbrella and planted herself in an upright canvas chair, with her legs crossed and her fingers knitted together in her lap. Her eyes were hidden behind sunglasses but you could tell from the grim scarlet set of her mouth that this was definitely not the way *she* would have chosen to spend Sunday – or indeed any other day. David's carrying on with the kids (ours included), she pretended not to notice. And, when it was time to eat, she made a show of ignoring him. Best of all, though, was when she asked Lois 'if it wouldn't be too much trouble' for her to have a 'proper plate'? It was 'silly', she supposed, but she had 'this thing about eating off plastic'. Somehow it worked out that Kelly was sent inside to fetch a china plate. Someone in the kitchen must have said something to her – because when she came back she asked Lois, 'Why's a person who has to have a special plate called a cunt?' Deirdre of course heard her, and that was that. Several people went over to try to talk to her but the only person who stayed with her any length of time was Lois.

Whether it was because David was showing Jeff how to make a fly for trout fishing out of a piece of cotton and a feather, or whether it was because she had made up her mind to sit it out for just so long and no longer (no migraines today; she was magnificent, the perfect lady, sterling silver and all the rest of it), at four o'clock on the dot Madam said in her grandest voice, 'David, I think it's time we were going now.'

'What already? I'm just showing Jeffrey how to tie a fly.'

'Your rest. You know how tired you get. If Elizabeth and Harrison don't mind, of course.'

'*My* rest?'

In the car she was fiercely silent while David looked kind of crumpled up. Madam was biding her time. First swipe, when it came, was at Liz. She was in the kitchen fixing dinner when in sailed Deirdre from her rest and said that, although she 'hated' repeating what other people had said, she considered it 'her duty as a sister-in-law' to tell Liz that Lois thought Jeff and Kelly go to bed far too late and that this is what makes them so rude and bad-tempered. 'Rude and bad-tempered?' Lois? Luckily, Liz realised just in time what she was up to, how she must have twisted whatever Lois had said in the hope of stirring up trouble between Lois and Liz, or possibly just to get some kind of reaction out of Liz. In any case, as David might have said, Liz wasn't 'rising to the bait'.

Next, over drinks and at dinner, in my usual role of the dumb American who had married David's sister, it was me. Usual sort of remarks about America and Americans, quite a bit about brunches and a reprise of David's monologue on the differences between European and American conversation. Having been warned by Liz though, I too refused to rise. So in the end it was David who got it, poor guy. He must have crashed out as soon as we got back from the brunch, so that she hadn't had a chance yet to tell him what she thought about his performance at Lois's. Or perhaps she had been saving it up for us, in case we should be in any doubt as to who wore the pants?

At any rate, after *her* performance at dinner, it was a pleasure to get out the card table. But whether David was still a bit hung-over from all those Bloody Bulls, or whether he had some idea of what was coming, he played still slower than ever. You could see her lips tightening, almost feel the temperature rising. For years she must have sat watching him drumming his fingers on the table, listening to his tuneless whistling. But now the pretence of a united front was suddenly thrown aside. 'For goodness' sake, David, can't you stop that awful whistling,' she hissed at him, as he pulled out a card, hesitated, put it back again. 'And that tapping too.'

David looked sheepish, mumbled, 'I'm sorry, I didn't realise', whistled a couple of sibilant notes and put down the three of trumps.

That did it.

'How many times have I told you?' squealed Madam Gracious, a luminous spot of crimson breaking through the surface of her make-up on either cheek. 'Never send a small boy in to do a man's work. If you're going to play a trump, play a high one.'

Of course she was right. At the end of the hand, since we had a game each, I suggested we break it off, carry on the next evening. Would anyone like a nightcap? No, they would not, Madam answered for both of them, and I shouldn't have liked to have been in David's shoes as she marched him off to bed.

April 6.
Day 7. Perhaps there is a God somewhere up there after all. This morning Liz called me at the office to say the Airline had made a hash of things. Either they would have to stay three extra days (Jesus!) or leave this afternoon. Went home for lunch. Everything hunky-dory. So sorry to have to leave in such a hurry. So marvellous to have seen us. We really must come to England soon. At the airport, we sent our love to Caroline and her clever husband and the perfect baby.

Just now Liz said to me, 'The moment you finish that diary of yours, I want it. This time I'm going to make sure Elspeth gets our version – and she should have some idea which one to believe after what *they* must have been through – before she gets Deirdre's.'

Seven

WEEKENDS

'The ideal guest shows his virtues in many subtle ways, but one of his salient qualities is that he is unpresuming.'
– Millicent Fenwick, *Vogue's Book of Etiquette*, 1948.

The Potters

Friday:

When Allan had told Judith about running into Jan Mallory at a party in London, she had been delighted. She had been pleased, too, that Allan, thinking Jan was looking rather low, had invited her and her husband (a man called Potter, who had not been at the party) for the weekend of the 3rd. The only slight problem was that the Potters would have to put up with Uncle Simon and Aunt Isobel at Sunday lunch: the date of this annual event had been fixed months ago, not only with the Uncle and Aunt, but with the vicar of a nearby village, who was one of the very few of her old friends whom Aunt Isobel still chose to recognise. But Jan had always been such a sweet-natured girl. And it was only one lunch. It must be twelve years now since the Mallorys had gone off to live in Italy, and Jan, who must have been about seventeen at the time, had disappeared from their lives.

Warned now by the shrill yapping of Mr Wilson that the Potters had arrived, Judith stuck the last stem of honeysuckle into the vase on what was to be the Potters' dressing table, and went over to the window. On the gravel below, a glistening green Volvo estate car scrunched to a halt. From Mr Wilson, a magnificent show of ferocity: yap, yap, yap, yap. But then, as a door was pushed cautiously open,

83

out leapt a labrador puppy – and there was poor old Mr Wilson flat on his back, his teeth bared in an ingratiating, lop-sided grin. The truth was out: Mr Wilson had bark but no bite. The puppy pranced about him in an ecstasy, bobbing down on his forelegs, sniffing at him, then tearing off again in another wild circle.

'Hm,' thought Judith, cupping a hand over the tortoiseshell butterfly which was flapping against the window pane, anxious to escape into the garden outside. A couple of weeks ago, Jan had telephoned to ask if it would be all right to bring their two children? Of course it would, Judith had said. Their own, who were away at school, were much older anyway. There was plenty of room. She just hoped they wouldn't be too bored. But nobody had said anything about a dog.

From the same door as the puppy there now emerged Jan, from the driver's side her husband, pulling off a pair of backless motoring gloves, and from behind a girl of about four and a boy of about seven. The girl had a gun in her hand.

'Magnus, stop it. Magnus, come here. Heel, Magnus,' Jan shouted at the uncomprehending puppy.

Judith pushed up the window, released the butterfly.

'It's all right,' she called out. 'Mr Wilson's quite used to it. I'll be down in a second.'

As she was crossing the hall, a chubby paw smashed through one of the panes of the inner hall door, the upper half of which was a window. Having brushed aside the splintered glass with her foot, Judith opened the door and in shot Mr Wilson, who made a bolt for the kitchen, pursued by the puppy, spattering blood as he went.

'Oh, I'm so sorry,' Jan said, seeing the trail of bloodstains on the stone floor. 'And the window too. How awful.'

'Don't worry,' Judith told her, instantly recognising what Allan had meant about her looking 'rather low'. From a plump, jolly teenager ('so outgoing for an only child,' people had always said), she seemed to have shrunk into one of those prematurely-aged, harassed housewives, whose glamorous friend is always telling her, on television, how to get her wash whiter, how to knock up a mouth-watering meal in three minutes flat, how to float through her day on a bubble of energy (out of a bottle: the product).

'I brought this,' Jan said. 'It isn't much. But I thought it might help.'

Judith found herself holding a casserole dish. She must have looked surprised.

'It's a rabbit stew.'

'Oh – how delicious.' Allan hated rabbit. Perhaps she could pretend it was chicken? Or decant it and keep it until after they were gone?

'And this is Tony,' Jan said, still looking flustered, as her husband came in with their suitcases. 'Oh, it *is* good to see you. Are you sure I couldn't get a cloth?'

'No, no, please don't bother. It's nothing.'

Judith slid the casserole on to the hall table, offered her hand to Tony.

'Nice place you've got,' said Tony, putting down the suitcases. 'Really, can't you stop him doing that?' He made a lunge behind Jan's back and pushed forward a thin, obviously very nervous little boy.

'Say hello, Ben,' said Jan coaxingly. 'This is Judith. An old friend of mine.'

The boy held out his hand, kept his eyes firmly on the ground.

'Come on now,' said Tony. 'Say hello properly.'

The hello was barely audible.

Tony patted the boy on the shoulder. 'Not like that. Say "Hello, Judith" – and how kind it is of her to ask you.'

'Hello, Ben,' Judith said quickly, taking the boy's hand. 'It's so nice of you to come.' But it was too late. The tears were already in his eyes and now he started to howl.

'Jesus!' said Tony.

'I'm so sorry,' said Jan, bending down to put her arms round the boy. 'I'm afraid he's a bit shy.'

'And whose fault is that?' said Tony. 'Mary, where are you? This is Judith, who's asked you to stay.'

'Hello, Judith,' said Mary and took careful aim at a point somewhere between Judith's eyes. There was a pop as the cork flew out of the gun on the end of its string.

'Got you,' said Mary. 'But you needn't lie down this time. Because I want you to show me where I'm going to sleep.'

'Oh dear,' said Jan. 'I'm afraid she's like that. I'm so terribly sorry.'

'There seems to have been a muddle,' said Allan, in bed. He had got down from London about an hour after the Potters' arrival, to find Tony sitting at his desk in the study, with his briefcase open in front of him, on the telephone.

'Won't be a minute,' Tony had said, and had been more than twenty.

'A muddle?'

'As if they'd been swopped over. The girl's more like a boy. And the boy's more like a girl.'

'Odd, isn't it? Poor Jan. She looks so crushed.'

'If only she'd stop apologising all the time.'

'I know. He's not much of a help, is he? With anything. Always getting at that wretched little boy. And at Jan.'

'What was all that fuss about not eating pork? He hasn't changed his name from Potstein, has he?'

Judith laughed.

'No. And he's not a Muslim either. At least not altogether. But it does have to do with spending so much time in the Gulf. He thinks pork's unclean. Full of tapeworms. And you should see the things she's brought down for those children to eat. The kitchen's stuffed with yoghurt and wheatgerm and all sorts of health food.'

'No wonder the boy looks so pasty.'

'But not the girl, you have to admit. In any case, she nearly drove Mrs Clarke mad. I told her we had plenty of eggs and fish fingers and things, and that

Mrs C. would be perfectly happy to make the children whatever supper they liked. But no, she didn't want to be "any trouble", she'd do it herself. And of course was a terrible nuisance. Kept chattering and asking where things were and generally getting under Mrs Clarke's feet. That's why dinner was so late.'

'Well, I hope Mrs C. doesn't give in her notice. The pork was particularly good, tapeworms or no.'

'What exactly does he do, did you gather?'

'Seems to sell valves and drilling equipment. He was quite interesting about the differences between the various Gulf States – even if he does think he's the greatest living authority on the Middle East. But I could have done without all that stuff about the wickedness of sending your children to private schools.'

'He did rather overdo it, didn't he?'

'Bloody rude – and, apart from anything else, I should have thought it was just what that boy needed.'

'Pretty offensive all round. What was all that telephoning about? He just marched into the study and got on with it.'

'Business. And I bet he's the sort who doesn't offer to pay for it. Where's that dog of theirs sleeping?'

'With them. Jan thought it would be best in a strange house. She'll get up and let it out, if it needs to be.'

'That's something, I suppose.'

'She was awfully upset about it breaking the window. Do you want me to have a word with her about the telephone?'

'Oh no, for Christ's sake don't. Let him make as many calls as he likes – anything rather than give her something else to apologise about.'

Saturday:

'I do hope you won't mind,' Jan asked Judith, looking more than usually apprehensive. 'It's an extraordinary coincidence really. I mean Tony had no idea he lived down here, this man he used to know in Qatar. He was in the tobacconist's with his wife. Tony's – I mean *we've* asked them for a drink. Before lunch.'

'Oh … er – how nice,' said Judith. 'What time?'

'Pretty soon, I should think,' Tony told her. 'I said why didn't they come straight along here when they'd finished their shopping? They know the village. Once they're here, it's not difficult to find the house, is it?'

'No,' said Judith. 'I'd better tell Allan.'

Allan, watched by Mr Wilson and Magnus, the puppy, was marking out the tennis court.

'What a nerve,' he said.

'Well, I suppose it might have been worse. I wouldn't have put it past him to ask a whole lot of people to lunch.'

'Perhaps he has? Look out – here he comes.'

'Attractive garden you've got here,' said Tony. 'Wouldn't mind something like it myself. If I had the time of course. But then I expect you have gardeners?'

'Not really,' Allan told him. 'Mrs Clarke's (that's the cook's) sons help with the heavy stuff. Luckily the younger one's a bit of a mechanic. And for the time being, at any rate, he's crazy about the mowing machine.'

'How convenient,' said Tony. 'And I suppose they help with that too?' He removed his pipe from his teeth, pointed it in the direction of the swimming pool.

'As a matter of fact, yes, he does.'

'And they use it,' put in Judith, fairly certain that she had caught the drift of what Tony was thinking, 'whenever they like.'

There was a sound of tyres on gravel, and Mr Wilson and Magnus were off in full cry through the orchard, up towards the house.

Tony stuck his pipe back into his mouth.

'How very neatly you seem to have got everything worked out,' he said.

Judith saw the look that came over Allan's face and intervened. 'That must be your friends,' she said. 'We'd better go on up.'

'Yes, you do that,' said Allan. 'I'll be with you in a minute. I'll just finish this.'

Not content with giving his friends (a retired major and his wife) drinks, Tony also insisted on taking them on a conducted tour of the house (pointing out furniture and pictures – 'they're particularly proud of this one' and 'naturally they inherited most of it' Judith overheard him saying), the stableyard, the garden and pool. They had been back in the drawing room about twenty minutes, were on their third gin and tonic, when the gong rang for lunch and the Major's wife sprang up from her seat.

'Great Scott,' she said, looking at her watch. 'It's half past one, Jimbo. Time we were making tracks.'

The Major consulted his own time piece, a fob-watch.

'One twenty-eight,' he said. 'To be precise. But you're right, of course. Mustn't outstay our welcome, what?'

'Oh, you haven't done that,' Judith told him. 'Really you haven't. It's just that we're rather in the cook's hands. She doesn't like to be kept waiting.'

'I should think not,' said the Major emphatically, knocking back the last of his 'G and T'. 'Ready then, wife?'

'Pretty ship-shape, eh, Jim?' said Tony, as they all went outside to say goodbye. 'I'm glad to have got you all together.'

'A marvellous surprise,' said Mrs Major. She took a card from her bag, gave it to Judith. 'Our vital statistics. I hope you'll drop in if you're passing. It's not that I don't have plenty to do of course, but sometimes I get quite lonely when Jimbo's away on his travels.'

'I daresay,' said Tony at lunch, 'you thought Jim Ibsell a pretty good bore?'

'Oh no,' said Judith. 'I wouldn't say that.'

'Well, I have to tell you,' Tony continued, ignoring her not altogether convincing protest, 'that he

probably knows more about the North Yemeni ascetics than anybody. No Oxford or Cambridge or
anything like that.' (Allan had been at Cambridge;
somehow it had come up the night before.) 'Comple-
tely self-taught. He's made them his life's work.'

'How interesting,' said Allan encouragingly. Much
better to listen to whatever Tony was obviously
determined to tell them about the North Yemeni
ascetics than to be drawn into another argument
about education or something like that. Just so long
as lunch would soon be over. The children were
eating with them and, although Ben was satisfactorily
silent, the sight of Mary shovelling lumps of food into

her gravy-smeared face was not an appealing one.
('Oh dear,' Jan said, doing her best to retrieve a
potato which was being battered to a pulp on the
table. 'I'm so sorry. I should have brought her high-
chair. *Please,* Mary, stop that. Try to eat properly.
Look – like Ben.' 'Because I like it this way,' said Mary,
plopping another potato on to the table, preparatory to
taking her spoon to it. 'And anyway Ben's wet. Ask
Tony – he's always saying how wet he is.')

91

'Well he's gone to bed,' Allan said, coming into his and Judith's bedroom with what was left of his whisky. 'And taken that bloody dog with him. I must say, it might have picked another rug to chew a great hole in.'

'Unfortunate,' Judith agreed. 'She was dreadfully upset though. She wanted to give us some money but I told her not to be silly. You don't think that man in World's End…'

'A hole that size?'

'No, I suppose not. Why were you so long?'

'He had a call to make.'

'At this time of night?'

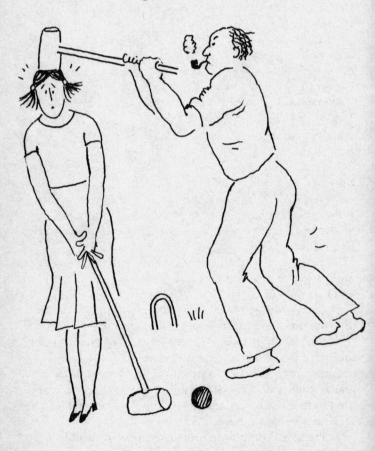

92

'To Singapore. Lucky we won that tenner off them at croquet.'

'That was odd, I thought. I mean his wanting to play for money. It didn't seem to fit.'

'Probably because he was sure he was going to win. He tried hard enough anyway. And bloody rude, I thought, to make all that fuss about having to play what *he* calls the "proper rules".'

'Didn't like losing it, did he? At one point it looked as if he was going to smash his mallet over poor Jan's head.'

'Contemptible. If he had done, I'd have smashed mine over his head. And broken that bloody pipe of his for good measure.'

'Allan!'

'It's the way he makes me feel. Why can't he let us answer the telephone in our own house? And how dare he go into the kitchen and give orders to Mrs Clarke?'

'Perhaps I shouldn't have told you about that?' Judith said. 'But at least Mrs C. seems to have simmered down. I don't think there will be any trouble.'

Sunday:

'What's that hanging out of the window?' Aunt Isobel asked querulously, hobbling along on the arm of Rogers, their chauffeur, while Judith followed behind with Uncle Simon.

'A bedcover,' Judith told her. 'It's the Potters', who are staying. Their dog had an accident in the night.'

'Dogs in bedrooms?'

'A puppy. It's all right now though. She's washed it out, she says. She must have put it there to dry.'

'Boarding house,' said Aunt Isobel. 'Potter, did you say? Do I know them?'

'You used to see her here years ago. As a child. Jan, you remember? The daughter of the Mallorys, who used to live in the Old Rectory.'

'Never heard of them.'

There was little point, Judith knew from experience,

93

in pressing such matters. 'Yesterday was too cold,' she said instead, 'but it's such a marvellous day today, they're all down by the tennis court. The children are swimming and Allan's made some Pimms. Or would you rather be inside?'

'Certainly not. Simon's got his hat. And I want to see the garden. We spend far too much time inside as it is.'

In the orchard they came across Mr Wilson, stretched out, panting, in the shadow of a pile of scythed grass. Having been taken thus by surprise, he decided it was too late to bark and heaved himself over on to his back, rolling his eyes at them.

'That the one?' Aunt Isobel asked, stopping to peer at him.

'No. That's Mr Wilson. Our dog.'

'I thought you said he was dead.'

'No. Not yet. He is eleven though.'

'What?' said Uncle Simon, who refused to wear a hearing aid.

'The dog,' said Aunt Isobel. 'It's not dead after all.'

'Of course it's not,' said Uncle Simon. 'I just saw it move.'

Allan and Tony were playing tennis, watched by the Vicar and Jan, who was cuddling Ben in her arms. Mary was splashing about in the pool.

'She doesn't remember you,' Judith warned Jan, before she introduced them. 'I'll just get a couple more chairs. But is Ben all right? He's shivering all over.'

'I'm afraid Tony got rather angry with him,' Jan explained. 'The thing is he's been trying to teach him to swim for ages and he just doesn't seem to be able to learn. Mary can of course, like a fish. But I think Ben's frightened of the water. Anyhow, he started to cry, so Tony threw him in.'

'How monstrous of him.'

'Well yes, I know, it was rather awful of him. I'm so sorry, Judith,'

'My dear girl,' Judith was surprised to hear herself say (it was not a phrase she was conscious of ever

94

having used before). 'What on earth have *you* got to be sorry about? Now come on, come and help me get some chairs, won't you, Ben, while Jan does the drinks?'

Reluctantly, the boy gave her his hand and they went over to the pool shed to bring back a chair each.

'Out,' shouted Allan. 'Thirty-all.'

'Are you sure?'

'It was fifteen-thirty, wasn't it?'

'I mean about it being out.'

'Pretty sure, yes.'

'It didn't look out from here.'

'Well, if you don't think so…'

'On the line, I'd have said.'

'Okay then, we'd better have it again.'

Allan served. An ace.

'Sun in my eyes,' said Tony, who went on to lose the game. As he and Allan were changing ends, he said he thought he'd like to have a go with another racket.

'You could try that one there,' Allan told him. 'Or you can have mine if you like? But quite honestly I think the one you've got is probably the best.'

'Couldn't be much worse anyway,' said Tony, ignoring Allan's offer of his own racket, but exchanging his for the one that had been lying under the net-winder. The thing was, of course, he was used to playing on hard courts. He hadn't played on grass for years now, he said.

'That man's losing,' said Aunt Isobel, pointing a trembling finger at Tony. 'And with very bad grace. Rotten sport.'

Tony whistled to himself, pretending not to have heard her.

'What's that?' said Uncle Simon.

'That man,' said Aunt Isobel. 'Palmer? Potts? A rotten sport.'

'Not a cloud in the sky,' said the Vicar. 'That rare thing nowadays, a real summer's day.'

Perhaps, Judith suggested, Aunt Isobel would like to see round the rest of the garden. And the Vicar too? It was at its best at the moment.

'Indeed I would,' said Aunt Isobel. 'Rogers can stay here and keep an eye on Simon.'

The tour of the garden must have taken about half an hour, with Aunt Isobel moving very slowly, exclaiming about this and that, one constantly-twitching arm hooked through Judith's and the other through the Vicar's. 'I was always a spring pruner myself,' she was saying, as they came round a clump of shrubs, back to the pool end of the tennis court. 'Good heavens, Judith!'

Allan told Judith later that Tony, having lost the last point of the match, had flung down his racket in disgust. What he 'could do with' was a swim. To Allan's astonishment – or was he so astonished? – he had started to strip off, there and then, on the court.

What now confronted Aunt Isobel, the Vicar and Judith was the sight of Tony stepping out of a pair of sweaty Y-fronts, which, as he straightened (it seemed defiantly) up, he kicked to one side, before diving into the pool.

'What's happened to Roger then?' Tony asked, looking round the dining room table.

'Rogers,' Aunt Isobel corrected him. 'No doubt he's having his lunch.'

'Not with us?'

Aunt Isobel looked at him in blank amazement.

'He's our chauffeur,' she said.

'Oh, I *see*,' said Tony, with a heavy sarcasm that was quite lost on Aunt Isobel. 'That explains everything.'

'Perhaps you'd like me to cut up your meat for you?' Jan said kindly, noticing how difficult Aunt Isobel's shakes made it for her to eat.

('Oh God, I should have told her,' thought Judith.)

'Certainly not,' said Aunt Isobel. 'I'm not absolutely gaga, you know. And it doesn't help at all to shout at Simon, either,' she told Tony, who had been doing just that.

'Delicious,' said the Vicar tactfully. 'I always say

your Mrs Clarke makes quite the best Yorkshire pudding.'

'Do you?' said Tony. 'Tell me, Vicar, how many people did you have in your church this morning?' And from that moment on nobody had any choice but to listen in silence, as Tony explained in detail to the Vicar how Christianity – and the Church of England, in particular – had got things wrong, whereas Mohammedanism, on the other hand, was getting so much right. Only once did he interrupt himself, and this was when Uncle Simon farted. 'And since when has a fart been funny?' he asked abruptly, rounding on Ben, who had been reduced to uncontrollable giggles. 'If you're going to behave like a snickering schoolgirl, get out. Go on, get out.'

Although Judith had made it as plain as she could that Sunday night was Mrs Clarke's night off and that their guests usually left on Sunday afternoon (the latter was not, in fact, strictly true), Tony had made it still more clear that it would suit him best to leave after supper, when there would be less traffic and the children could sleep in the car. They could have Jan's rabbit stew, couldn't they?

So, after tea and Uncle Simon and Aunt Isobel's departure, they had sat down again in the drawing room and Allan and Judith had pretended to be absorbed in the Sunday papers. Ben and Mary, meanwhile, had been taken upstairs to the old nursery, to play with the few remaining toys that had not already been broken by other visiting children. When, at last, it was time to heat up the inescapable rabbit (Judith had thought it best to warn Allan about this: in case he should say something about it that might hurt Jan's feelings), Jan had insisted on going with her into the kitchen, where, in her eagerness to be helpful, she had been nothing but a nuisance. Then, somehow, the six of them had got through their shares of the peculiarly tasteless rabbit (with lentils), had eaten raspberries from the garden with cream and some Stilton: and it was time for the Potters to leave.

When Mary said she would like to come again, both Allan and Judith affected not to have heard her.

'Ah well,' said Tony, his pipe firmly between his teeth. 'Expect we'll see you in London, eh?'

'It was wonderful,' said Jan. 'I can't thank you enough. I'm just so sorry about the rug … and the window …'

'Never mind,' Judith told her firmly. The list could have been a long one. 'These accidents do happen.'

Tony was revving the engine.

'You're so sweet, so understanding,' murmured Jan, obeying his summons.

'Like hell I am,' said Judith, as she and Allan stood side by side, waving at the tail lights of the car. 'If she only knew how close I came to screaming at her this evening. I mean how can she be so hopeless? Why doesn't she stand up for herself? Ever?'

'Do you think,' Allan wondered, 'they did anything about Mrs C.? If not, you know, we'd better.'

'I certainly didn't see him give her anything,' Judith said. 'But perhaps he left something in the room. I'll go and look. Also check that they didn't leave anything.'

Allan had gone back into the dining room for a last glass of port, was coming out again with it, when he heard a yell from Judith.

'What on earth was that?' he shouted up the stairs.

'Needless to say, they've left nothing,' Judith shouted back at him. 'But Mr Wilson – you filthy dog.' (Dull thump of flesh on fur.) 'Filthy! He's just peed all over the bed. Where that brute of theirs left *his* tip for Mrs C.'

At that moment the telephone rang.

'I'll get it,' Allan said, and went into the study.

'Will Mr Tony Potter,' a female voice asked him, 'take a collect call from Caracas?'

'No,' said Allan. 'He will not.' And banged down the receiver.

Eight

A FEW DAYS IN THE CITY

'There is almost nothing that a guest can do that is
worse than making himself too obviously at home in
a house that belongs to someone else.'
– Millicent Fenwick, *Vogue's Book of Etiquette*, 1948.

The Godson
*Here (with the kind permission of the authoress) is the
first and longer part of a letter written by Elaine Tronson, of
New York City, to her brother Leo and his wife Susie, who
live in Kyoto, Japan.*

N.Y.C.
15 th April.

Dear Susie and Leo,

If it wasn't for all the talk right now about
economising, I should almost certainly have called
you – not just to say 'Happy Easter' to you all (Happy
Easter!), but more, I'm afraid, to get my 'godson' off
my chest. As it is, though, I'm trying to be good (no
sign as yet of any alimony; attorney says be patient: I
try to be patient; work? – can't complain, and more
money, they say, next year). So a letter, and a long
whining one it will be.

It all started in January when I did one of my talks
in Orlando and afterwards up came Grace Wolfe. Did
you meet them ever? They were our neighbours in
Mobile, and Frank and I saw a lot of them at that
time. Naturally, I was pleased to see her after all these
years. I said how sad it was we'd lost touch after we'd
moved up to New York, told her about Frank's and
my divorce, asked how long they'd been living in
Orlando, how her husband and her kids were doing?
The usual sort of thing. And that's when I remembered I was supposed to be the godmother – Grace

used to be a great church-goer – of one of her boys. I never knew quite what it meant, to do with giving him bibles and things like that I think, so I said I hadn't done much about it, had I, and now it was probably a bit late? Well, it just so happened it wasn't. The kid – Jody was his name – had just dropped out of his art course, at the moment he was working in a store, but he longed more than anything to visit Manhattan. Perhaps in the spring, when the weather got warmer? He could bring a sleeping bag. I told her I could do better than that, I would give him my guest-room. It was a pity, she said, I couldn't meet him. But, as I was going on to Naples the same day, I gave her a card and told her just to let me know when.

So CUT, as they say in the movie business, to about three weeks ago, when Grace calls and asks me how am I fixed? Jody has managed to hold down his job for nearly four months but now it's finished and she thinks it would be good for him to spend a few days in the City, to see the museums and that sort of thing. Fine, I said, I was leaving soon to do a project on the West Coast. Why didn't he come up a couple of days before I left, so that I could show him round a bit and then he could have the place to himself? If that was all right by her?

It was. And that's the last thing that's been all right about it. To begin with, he was supposed to arrive around dinner time, which would have given me time to get things ready and fix something to eat. But no. At four-thirty I get a call at work from one of the elevator men. There are a couple of kids in the hall who say doesn't he have a key to my apartment and can't he let them in? Name of Wolfe. A couple of kids? Perhaps he'd come up with a brother or something? Okay, I said, let them in. Tell Jody to make himself at home. I'll be home as soon as I can after six.

CUT again – to around 6.30. The moment I stepped out of the elevator I was as good as knocked off my feet by the throb of music blasting down the hallway from my apartment. And when I got inside, there he was, my 'godson', lying full length on the chesterfield, with his boots planted on the arm and a girl sitting beside him, bent over him.

What with the music and the rest of it, they hadn't heard me. Until it's happened to you, you won't believe how weird it is to come into your apartment and feel like someone who shouldn't be there. In the end the only thing I could think of doing was to go over to the record-player and turn down the sound a bit. At this the girl jumped up and just stood there staring at me, with great poppy eyes, like a rabbit. Then he got up – very slowly, I can see it now – and turned round to face me. He's large, without being well-built (thick hips, legs too short for his body), not in any way good-looking (springy not very clean hair, puffy face and sharp little close-together eyes), and yet, I don't know why, he seems to have this strange confidence, as if he's sure that he's somehow special and you're going to be bowled over by him.

'Hi,' he said, with a cat's whiskery sort of a smile that was more condescending than friendly. He didn't bother to come over or shake hands or anything like that. 'You must be Mum's friend Elaine.' He pointed to the girl. 'This is Carole.'

So I said 'Hi' to them and 'glad you got here okay', or something dumb like that. Grace hadn't mentioned anything about a girlfriend, but it was obvious enough he expected her to stay with him. And in a way it seemed a good thing. At least they'd have each other for company. (It wasn't till later I found out they'd picked each other up on the bus on the way here. He was telling her how he'd got a cheap week's visit ticket by travelling at an off-peak time and somehow it all came out.) Still, I wanted him to know I didn't like his assuming that he could just land her on me like that without warning, so I told them to help themselves to anything they liked from the refrigerator while I got *his* room ready, then I'd get *him* some dinner.

He didn't seem to notice this. But the rabbit did.

Her eyes opened so wide I thought they'd fall out. So, feeling sorry for, I asked her if she'd like to stay and have something to eat with us? No answer. Those panicky eyes of hers were fixed on him, Jody.

'Perhaps Carole would like to stay to dinner?' I asked him.

'Dinner?' he said. 'Oh sure. She's with me, I guess.'

The poor girl looked so relieved I didn't say any more. What was the good of torturing her, I thought, when he couldn't see – or didn't want to see? – that I was trying to get at him? By the time I'd made up the guest beds and prepared dinner for them, though, while they sat like a couple of lumps on the chester-field, he drinking beer from the can and getting up every few minutes to turn over or change records (none of which he much liked, *that* was obvious), she sipping coke and flicking through old magazines – by then I felt pretty much the same way about her as I did about him.

Nor during dinner did either of them do anything to make me any keener on them. From her, a question repeated several times might with luck get an occasional, scarcely audible word or two for an answer; but if she was too nervous, or simply too dumb, to know what to say, he was at first too busy stuffing food into his mouth and then, when that was over, he made it perfectly plain that he just couldn't be bothered to make the effort. So, while I did the dishes, she went back to the magazines – she must have looked through each one of them at least twenty times – and he, after putting on and taking off a few more records, asked me didn't I have a T.V.? As you know it's in my bedroom, so I got it out and the two of them sat in front of it – he sprawled out with his feet on the coffee table, she all hunched up and awkward, with her mouth open – flipping from one program to another, saying absolutely nothing to me and almost nothing to one another.

Well, after about an hour of that, I said I was going to bed and perhaps they'd like to see their room and what about the next day, what did they plan on doing, which museum or whatever? – I'd show them how to get there on a map which I'd give them.

I might have known better, I suppose. Jody certainly had no intention of looking like 'some crumby tourist, with a street-plan'. He'd find his way about okay. Probably take cabs. Anyway, he didn't know what he'd be doing yet.

At all this talk of what *he* would or would not be doing, the girl of course started looking rattled again; so I gave him a set of keys and showed her where the breakfast things were – since it didn't seem to me likely they'd be up before I left for work. (And was I right? When I called at lunch time to find out about their dinner plans, anyone could have told that he'd still been asleep.) Then I showed her their room and the bathroom and their towels and so on, and said that if they didn't have anything to do tomorrow evening I'd make a *lasagne* which we could all eat at about nine: all they needed to do was to call me at the office in the morning and let me know. Oh yes, and I told them too that, if they found anything was short, to call the corner grocery and charge it to my account.

'Fine,' was the best he could do; but the rabbit did manage to get out 'Thanks' and even, when I shut the glass doors between the corridor and the sitting room, 'Goodnight'.

As I had a meeting in the morning and was leaving for Los Angeles the day after, I took a couple of nembuthal and went out like a sack of potatoes.

CUT to Wednesday evening. When I'd called from work he'd said he *thought* they'd be in for dinner; so I'd gone round the block to the little Italian store to buy fresh pasta and the rest of it. I'd also told him again nine, because I had to be up early to catch my plane. He'd said that was fine. So it came as a bit of a surprise when the elevator man told me they'd had a delivery of groceries at about five and only gone out a few minutes ago. 'Funny kids,' the elevator man said. 'The girl looks kind of scared, as if she'd seen a ghost or something.'

Well, she'd have had good reason to look scared, I

can tell you, if she'd been there when I got into the apartment. For a start, the dining table was still covered with the debris of their meal: mugs with filmed-over coffee in them, a couple of beer cans, egg-smeared plates, half a scrunched-up French loaf, crumbs everywhere and gobs of jelly stuck to the table. In the sink were a couple of greasy frying pans and, when I opened the refrigerator, I found a whole lot of my stuff had been taken out to make room for two shelves full of beer. Worse still was the bathroom: round the bath was a glutinous band of scum and tightly-curled pubic hairs (his, I reckoned); in the plughole of the sink a wad of longer, lighter hairs (hers?); at the back of the sink squeezed-out lengths of toothpaste and a topless tube oozing more paste; the carpet soaking wet, all the towels also soaking (mine included) and left in a heap on the floor; and one more thing – you can imagine what – too disgusting to describe. (Perhaps Grace is too busy with her church-going, I remember thinking, to have had time to teach her kids to use a toilet brush?)

Their bedroom, too, looked as if the same tornado had hit it, with a few more beer cans and clothes and bedclothes strewn all over it. But worst of all was when I came to look more closely at the mess I'd already noticed scattered about the chesterfield and on the coffee table. It turned out they'd been making some kind of collage, so that the floor was littered with snippings and torn-out magazine pages; and there pasted in among all the other junk – Christ knows what was the point of the thing – were bits of photographs cut out of the one and only dummy copy of my new summer lecture hand-out (which I was pretty sure, but not altogether sure, had been shut away in my desk). At first I felt like screaming. So I did. Then I realised that the rest of the dummy must be somewhere in the pile of garbage on the floor.

It seems strange now but by the time I'd salvaged what was left of the forty-odd pages – about a third of them were still intact – I felt much better. It was like finishing a puzzle. And, maybe, also, a couple of drinks had something to do with it? Anyway, I locked the remains of the dummy into the desk and, after I'd cleared the dining table and was fixing dinner, decided that not having had any kids of my own – and not even seen that much of other people's – I must have become like one of those awful old spinsters whose obsession with routine and tidiness is their whole life. For some reason this made me feel better about them too: so that when they hadn't shown up by nine-thirty, and I sat down with a bottle of wine to some *lasagne,* I was almost grateful to them for this timely reminder.

In the meantime I'd worked out what I was going to say. And when they came in at about a quarter of ten (with a load of records but no apology, of course), I gave them their dinner and said it. The dummy wasn't mentioned: as I said, I couldn't be certain it hadn't been lying around, and besides, since there was nothing they could do about it now, I thought it would have been not only pointless but petty. (My new self!) What I did say, though, was that I was very busy at the moment and hadn't had the time to wash their dishes; that there was no maid, so would Carole please see to all that sort of thing while I was away; and that when they left on Tuesday could they please have a special clear-out, so that I wouldn't have to do it for them when I got back that evening?

Throughout all this Jody looked at me with a kind of uncomprehending amazement, as if I'd suddenly launched into a résumé of Lenin's politics or the sex life of the fruit-fly. But at least I seemed to have got through to the girl: because there and then (to *my* atonishment) she volunteered to do the dinner dishes; and in the morning, before I left, I noticed that although the bath hadn't been cleaned, the rest of the bathroom was in fairly good order and all the rubbish from the making of the collage had been bundled into the trash-can. So off I went, greatly reassured.

CUT to yesterday morning, when I arrived back in the City on the red-eye. (Everything in California went off fine. Saturday and Sunday with friends in

106

Palm Springs.) I'd called the apartment once and got Carole, who told me – in her mumbly, monosyllabic way – that they were having 'a good time'. No problems? 'No.' So it was, as they say, 'without any qualms' that I went back to the apartment to pick up the remains of the dummy which I'd left in the desk and would have to be put together again by the end of the week to be on schedule for the printers. I told the cab to wait.

At once, from the look on the elevator man's face, I knew something was wrong. 'Trouble?' 'Big trouble. They made such a racket the neighbours started calling down and Lewis had to go up and tell them to cut it out. More trouble. But you know Lewis. He got most of them out of there, I guess.'

'Most of them?'

'That's what Lewis said. He thought there were probably more of them in the bedrooms. But since he couldn't get in there and the row stopped, he reckoned he'd done okay.'

'Well, thank him for me anyway, will you?' I said. 'And I'll see him later. Do you think he'll remember who called down?'

When we got to my floor, he asked me if I'd like him to come along with me? In case? I told him 'No', I could handle it. If he'd just pay off my cab for me? It wasn't until I tried to fit my key into the hole that I realised I was trembling. But that was rage.

Inside the drapes were pulled and it was still dark. I switched on the lights. Both my own bedroom and the guest room were locked, so I banged on the doors and went into the living room. Here the furniture had been pushed out of the way, the rugs pulled up and Carole was asleep, fully dressed, on the chesterfield. The place smelled like the inside of one of those club ashtrays with a revolving lid. All over the place there were scattered pillows and cushions, beer cans, half empty glasses, saucers full of cigarette butts, the odd bit of clothing; in the kitchen, amongst the piles of dirty dishes, more glasses, cheese rinds and a couple of charred sausages sitting in a pan of white solidified

fat, a cigarette had burnt itself out on the work surface, leaving a long black scar in the wood.

'What the hell's been going on?' I yelled at Carole, shaking her. She must have been pretending to be asleep, because straight away she started to wail. She seemed to be saying something about Jody and 'guys'. What 'guys' I wanted to know, and what was Jody doing locked up in one of my rooms?

Well, that was just it, it turned out. It seems Jody had gone gay on her and locked himself into my room with beer and poppers and a pair of boys. 'I'm not surprised,' I'm afraid I told her, and left her there snivelling, to go and bang on my bedroom door. When at last Jody said he'd be out in a minute, I went on to the guest-room. 'Who the fuck's that?' a girl's voice asked me from inside. 'This is the owner of this apartment, that's who,' I screamed back, by now so mad I'd as good as lost control. 'If you're not out of there and out of this building in five minutes, I'm calling the police.' 'Shit,' said a man's voice. 'I guess it really is.' Then louder, to me: 'Okay lady, we're going. Don't lose your cool.' 'Five minutes,' I yelled back at him and went into the bathroom.

If the rest of the apartment was a mess, the bathroom was something else again. It looked like an entire football team had been through the place, and on top of that all my make-up had been got down from the shelves and thrown about. Wedged behind the bath taps there was a hypodermic and in the bath itself slivers of broken glass. While I was trying to pick these out, I heard a noise behind me and just caught a glimpse of a bearded man and a girl making a dash for the front door. A moment later two guys shot out of my room, grabbed some things from the sitting room and followed the others out.

'Okay, Jody,' I yelled, yanking a wet bra and some knickers down off the shower rail. 'You can pack your bags and get out.'

'But you said you'd be back this evening,' he said, coming out into the corridor.

'Well, here I am, aren't I?' I told him. 'Just get your things together and go.'

'But what …?' I don't know what he was going to say. 'Just go,' I shouted, and threw the bra and knickers at him. 'Both of you. At once.'

Carole, still sniffing, was banging things about in the kitchen area.

'I'll help you,' she said. 'No, you won't,' I told her. 'I'm late for work as it is. You'll get out. And I'll clear up this filth this evening.'

'But I can't go. Not now. Not with him.'

'Oh yes, you can.'

Since she didn't seem able to move, I took hold of her and steered her – quite gently, I think – across the living room and into their bedroom. 'Pack. Quickly. And go.'

'Well,' Jody began confidently, indeed almost aggressively, a couple of minutes later, coming towards me with his holdall hanging from one shoulder. The girl was a step behind him, carrying a small suitcase, hovering.

'Well nothing,' I told him. 'Just get out. The pair of you.'

He seemed to hesitate for a second or two but then went, with her trundling along in his wake, like a wooden doll, with her arms hanging stiffly at her sides and the little suitcase dangling from one of them.

I was about to leave myself when a thought struck me. I called the corner store, gave them the dates. They called me back later, at work. Four hundred and eighty-six dollars! A whole evening spent cleaning up yesterday! And still more to do now!

At this point Ms. Tronson goes on to give news of her and Leo's parents and other family matters. But the postscript to her letter reads as follows:-

P.S.

After a good deal of thought about what to say (and more about what not to say), have just called Grace Wolfe in Orlando. Either Jody is back there already or he must have called her: and told her some *quite* different story. After a few reasonably abusive remarks – I didn't get a chance to say anything beyond giving my name – she told me she was sorry Jody and I hadn't 'got along together'. Then hung up on me.

Nine

GRATITUDE

> 'Gratitude is a burden upon our imperfect nature,
> and we are but too willing to ease ourselves of it, or
> at least to lighten it as much as we can.'
> – Lord Chesterfield, Letter to his Godson, Philip
> Stanhope, November 7, 1765.

To some people, saying thank you – and looking and
sounding as if they mean it – comes easily. To others
it doesn't. Indeed, there are men and women who find
it impossible to look anyone who gives them a present
in the face. This is a disadvantage in life: because,
although there are also people (often the same people)
who don't like to be thanked for things, the majority
of human beings do. It is after all only natural that

anyone who has gone to some trouble or expense, should prefer that that trouble (and to a lesser degree, as a rule, the expense) should not be taken for granted. Whatever may have been said in recent years to the contrary, the person who behaves as if he had a God-given right to his neighbour's ox, ass or what-have-you, is still not a popular one – at least not with his neighbours.

Saying thank you, then, is an important duty of anyone who receives a present or favour, and most especially of the guest who has enjoyed the liberality of someone else's table or house. Nor need a guest's expression of his appreciation be limited to mere verbal thanks. Since the much lamented decline in the number of servants to be had for a reasonable price, it has become quite common for guests at a dinner party to send a postcard or letter to thank their host and hostess, particularly when these have cooked and served the meal themselves. Strictly speaking, though, according to the most up-to-date authorities, for a dinner party a telephone call will suffice.

In the case of an overnight stay, on the other hand, a letter – and not just a postcard – is obligatory. 'Bread-and-Butter Letters', writes Millicent Fenwick in *Vogue's Book of Etiquette*, 'must be written when one has spent a night or more in someone's house.' And although such letters 'may be varied in infinite ways to cover an infinite number of circumstances, the form of a bread-and-butter letter is supposed to be as

113

follows: in the first paragraph, thanks and expressions of one's enjoyment of the visit; in the second, a short anecdote or a phrase or two about one's trip home, or something else indirectly connected with the visit; in the third, renewed thanks.'

In such letters 'the wit must be personal'. As an illustration 'of the form and the general tone' that a bread-and-butter letter (to a contemporary) should take, Ms. Fenwick offers:

'Dear Evie,

Thank you so much for the wonderful week end. We so loved seeing you and Harry again, and we couldn't have enjoyed ourselves more.

Our arrival home was clouded by the news that every chicken had escaped from the coop and, although it was by then eleven o'clock, Louis felt it necessary to make efforts to retrieve them from the trees where they were roosting. I missed the peace of our week end very much indeed!

I hope we shall see you both very soon. Louis sends you his love, with many thanks again from us both,

Affectionately,
Muriel.'

For 'a whole weekend visit,' Letitia (Tish) Baldridge, in *The Amy Vanderbilt Complete Book of Etiquette*, prescribes something rather longer. On 'your best stationery', it should be easy 'to fill two or three pages with reminiscences and observations on the meals, activities, the people you met, the nice house and so on.' In her days as social secretary at the White House, Ms. Baldridge 'found it fascinating to observe the flow of beautiful, personal handwritten notes sent by Mrs. John F. Kennedy to her hostesses the day after a party she and the President had attended, as well as the letters sent to Mrs. Kennedy by Mrs. Lyndon Johnson, Mrs. Harry Truman, and Mrs. Dwight Eisenhower, each after having been individually received at the White House. If the First Ladies of the land, past and present,' she says, 'have the manners and discipline to make time to put pen

114

to paper, in order to say thank you, then the rest of us should be able to do it too.'

Next comes the question of presents, the giving of which does not (as some people suppose) exonerate the donor from his or her obligation either to write or say thank you. 'If you have been the guest of honor at a party, or if you have been a weekend guest,' writes Letitia Baldridge, 'you really should send or bring your hosts a joint gift.' In the case of the 'guest of honor,' it has become increasingly usual to send flowers to the hostess beforehand, so that they can be on display at the party – a practice which seems to have originated in North Germany and the Scandinavian countries. As to presents for weekend visits, all modern writers on etiquette and manners are agreed that these should be 'suitable' (live birds, fish and animals are particularly to be avoided; to send a cookery book to a host or hostess who has served up a succession of disgusting meals would be a mistake). General favourites are chocolates, candy, flowers, pot plants, felt pens, place mats, soap and sets of guest towels.

'You are a shooting man, and your visit has been to a town house? A brace of grouse,' suggest the Experienced Hands who wrote *Tips on Tipping* (1933), 'or a brace of pheasants – or two brace – would be a nice attention. A leg of mutton, which would cost more, would be rude. Game is polite.... Trout and salmon you may send, but not cod; a hare, but not a couple of rabbits, except in extreme cases.... If you are a fisherman, even to a shooting house a grilse or a dish of trout is a pleasing attention, and if you are a countryman and your hostess is the town bird, a basket of peaches, or a bag of walnuts, or a hamper of decent plums or apples or peas warms many hearts. If you come from the Stilton neighbourhood, or from Cheddar way, or from Wensleydale, a cheese you have "picked up" is a handy piece of luggage to unload on your hostess, and later on tickets for the ball she wouldn't otherwise go to, or a box at the theatre, are very grateful tickles to a, perhaps, middle-

115

aged hostess who feels she is merely looked upon as
the landlady of a free public-house'.

More original, possibly, are some of Letitia Baldridge's suggestions. What about 'a saucy little bell,
in porcelain, crystal or silver – to use as a table bell,
but useful also for someone who is sick in bed;
laminated plastic canapé trays; a jar of freshly made
(and freezable) spaghetti sauce'; or '(for hot-weather
entertaining) votive candles set in all kinds of decora-
tive holders, including hanging garden lamps'? Or
some people might prefer to follow Elizabeth L. Post's
advice and give their weekend hosts 'a pair of *good*
scissors'.

In a household where there are children, it is
apparently permissible to bring presents for the
children, and not for the parents. Once again live-
stock is out. But money, which must not of course be
offered to a host or hostess (unless there is an
agreement to share· costs), may be safely given to
children (provided they are not 'fagged' or made to
run errands for it).

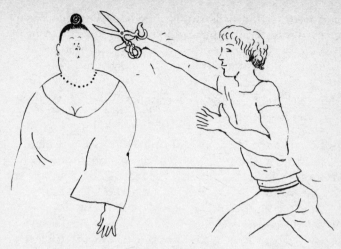

To servants, money has to be given – as a tip. With one proviso: if the guest knows the servant well, it might 'give a great deal more pleasure' to bring a present such as 'candy or a scarf' for the maid, 'pipe tobacco or a defroster for the windshield of his car' for the butler (Millicent Fenwick). The dictionary definition of a tip is 'a small present of money given to an inferior; a gratuity, a douceur'. Perhaps, the Experienced Hands wonder, the word may derive from tipple? In France, after all, there is *le pourboire,* in Spain *la propina,* in Germany *das trinkgeld.* In the seventeenth century, Samuel Pepys 'did give' to an old man who had brought him some letters 'a bottle of Northdown ale, which made the poor man almost drunk'.

Be that as it may, few people today would welcome a guest who left their staff 'almost drunk'. Far better money. But not too much of it. 'The vulgar, self-advertising person who throws money away in tips … is an offence to the tipping community. So far from gaining any respect, he is regarded with contempt even by the recipients of his largesse.' Thus the Experienced Hands. 'Some poeple have an entirely wrong idea about tipping,' wrote Lady Troubridge, in 1931, 'and think that they must give an amount proportionate to the style of the establishment they

117

are visiting. This is a mistake. Tips should be given in accordance with one's own means, and it is foolish of people to give tips beyond what they can afford.'

In Lady Troubridge's day, for a weekend visit to 'a house where a butler and footman are kept', 'a fair amount' for a man to have given would have been 10s. (50p) to the butler, 5s (25p) to the valet if he valets him, 2s. 6d. (12½p) to the chauffeur who drives him to and from the station. A single woman, however, would not need to give the housemaid more than '2s. 6d. to 3s. 6d.' – although, 'if a visitor gives much trouble, her tips should be higher'.

More recently (1980), Charlotte Ford has suggested that 'if you're weekending in a house with a fairly large staff it's best to tip everyone two or three dollars at the end of your stay: for instance, two dollars to the cook, two dollars to the person who took care of your room, and two dollars to the person who brought you your breakfast and who sees to the comfort of the house.' As to the actual giving of these tips, 'You may put each separate amount in an envelope with each person's name on it and leave them with your host, or, if you know them well, give the envelope directly to each person.'

A few people still ask their guests not to tip their servants; in which case it's bad manners to do so. But most employers – and servants – expect tips. At shooting parties and on yachts, there is often a set scale. If in doubt as to how much to give, the thing to do is to ask the host or hostess. As Letitia Baldridge says: people 'with a staff are used to the question; you won't be the first to ask it'.

Having brought presents, tipped the servants, said thank you and written a bread-and-butter letter, there still remains the question of reciprocity. 'A cutlet for a cutlet' is a principle to which many people today would claim not to subscribe. It sounds somehow cheap; tit-for-tat; niggling. Yet, although there does exist a breed of compulsive party-givers, gregarious and open-handed individuals or couples, who like to feel that every chair in their dining room, every

room in their house, is being put to maximum use, even these in the end seem to expect some sort of cutlet. True, if you are a 'star', or can sing for your supper in some other way, you may get away without producing it; you may even be allowed to return home from your weekend with carrier bags full of garden produce and what is left of the Puligny Montrachet '62 – and sit there, consuming it, while confidently waiting for the telephone to ring with your next invitation.

Generally speaking, though, the life of the sponger is an invidious one. He must forever be on the alert for new victims on whom to fasten, when, as nearly always happens, his present benefactors grow tired of him. And so too, sooner or later, must the kind of person whose idea of repaying a year's round of dinners, dances and weekends is to throw an annual cocktail party; or, worse still, in many ways, two of these, on consecutive evenings, so as to economise on the hired glasses, the flowers and the canapés. (The cold leftovers from the first night's shindig are tarted up with a new coating of mayonnaise and the hot ones reheated, yet again, for the second night.) Not that everybody expects exactly the same size or shape of cutlet in return for their own. As with tips and presents, the nature of the reciprocal gesture will be dictated – quite correctly, in Lady Troubridge's view – by means and circumstances. But shabbiness is always recognizable as shabbiness. It is ungracious. It is discourteous. And – the pundits are all agreed on this – it just will not do.

The Perfect Guest

She answered by return of post
The invitation of her host.
She caught the train she said she would,
And changed at junctions as she should.
She brought a light and smallish box
And keys belonging to the locks.
Food, strange and rare, she did not beg,
But ate the homely scrambled egg.
When offered lukewarm tea she drank it.
She did not crave an extra blanket,
Nor extra pillows for her head:
She seemed to like the spare-room bed.
She never came downstairs till ten.
She brought her own self-filling pen,
Nor once by look or word of blame
Exposed her host to open shame.
She left no little things behind,
Excepting ... loving thoughts and kind.

Rose Henniker Heaton